— • —

Yesterday's Soil
Today's Faith
Tomorrow's Bloom

— • —

Resilient ROOTS

Resilient ROOTS

A Memoir

First Edition

ISBN: 979-8-9945367-0-4 (Paperback)
Cover Design by Halaina
Published by Halaina
Myrtle Beach, South Carolina
Printed in the United States of America
This is a work of nonfiction. Names, places, and certain identifying details have been changed to protect the privacy of individuals.

DEDICATION

To the unseen roots
that held when the ground gave way,
and to the light
that stayed until I rose.

EPIGRAPH

Oh Ramallah, city of my longing,
how distant you feel when I am gone.
I speak to you as if you can hear me,
as if the heart can travel where the body cannot.
Life has carried me far.
It never loosened your hold on my soul.
Every road that led me away
carved your name deeper into me.
Ramallah,
you are not only a place—
you are memory,
breath,
ache,
and home.
Even when I leave,
I am still walking within you.

Author's Note

This memoir contains experiences of domestic violence, sexual assault, and trauma.

I have told this story as truthfully as I could. Some moments may be difficult to read.

Names and identifying details have been changed to protect the privacy of those involved.

If any part of this story feels close to your own, you are not alone.

Support is available:

National Domestic Violence Hotline:

1-800-799-7233 (SAFE)

TTY: 1-800-787-3224

www.thehotline.org

TABLE OF CONTENTS

INTRODUCTION

"Tell me your story."

I've said it thousands of times in my salons in South Carolina and Virginia.

Most women smile. Some hesitate. A few laugh it off.

But every once in a while, someone goes quiet—and then says something they've never said out loud before.

That's the moment I wait for—when the truth finally slips through.

I've spent years holding other people's stories—listening without judgment, without interruption, without looking away.

What I didn't know was how much it would cost me to keep avoiding my own.

Because where I come from, silence isn't just a habit.

It's survival.

I grew up in the hills of Ramallah, in a world where questioning anything—your family, your faith, your place—wasn't just discouraged. It wasn't allowed.

There were nights the curfew fell like a held breath over the whole city. Doors closed. Streets emptied. The world outside went still in a way that didn't feel like peace—it felt like warning. I would lie in the dark as a girl and listen, straining to understand what was out there, what it wanted, when it would end.

It never told me. That was the point.

You learned not to ask. You learned not to move. You learned that safety lived in smallness—in taking up as little space as possible, making as little noise as you could.

But there was Maha.

My sister was always a step ahead of me—in the classroom, on the road to school, in the way she understood things before I had found the words for them. Walking beside her each morning was the one place the world felt navigable. She taught me without making me feel small. She pointed things out—a word, an idea, a way of seeing—and waited for me to catch up.

She was the only person who made me feel like my voice was worth something.

I carried both of those things out of Ramallah.

The fear that had taught me to go quiet. And the memory of what it felt like to be heard.

After a while, I didn't just hide my voice.

I lost it.

This book is the story of finding it again.

Not in one moment. Not cleanly. But slowly—through salons and marriages and grief and open roads and children who grew up watching me figure out how to stand.

Through loss that hollowed me. Through love that showed me what I deserved. Through mornings that kept coming even when I wasn't sure I wanted them to.

If you have ever gone quiet to survive—if you have ever made yourself smaller so someone else could feel larger—this story is for you.

Tell me your story. And let me tell you mine.

Chapter 1

OPENING GROUND

"The Lord will provide."
(Genesis 22:14, NIV)

I was born into a house still waiting for that to be true.

Food was rationed. Space was shared. The house knew how to be careful because it had to be.

Yamma, my mother was awake before dawn. As a girl in braids, she ran barefoot through sun-warmed courtyards, her laughter quick and sharp. Morning found her beside her mother, hands wrapped around the wooden handle, grinding wheat against stone.

School was never part of her world. Girls were meant to go—but not Yamma. Not in my family.

Each morning came with chores. Water carried, dough kneaded, floors swept before the sun climbed too high.

By fourteen, the lightness in her steps had thinned. Her laughter came less often, then not at all. Her shoulders settled into a discipline that did not loosen. She was married soon after.

The match was arranged behind closed doors, discussed in private rooms, her name spoken more often than her voice, and decided without her being heard. By the time she crossed the threshold of her husband's home, everything had already been settled.

She entered to serve her husband, moving carefully within his family—measuring what she said, where she stood, how much space she was allowed to take. Respect was expected in the way she spoke, the way she lowered her eyes.

Obedience wasn't questioned. It showed in pauses, in glances, in how the house listened.

Daughters were raised with one foot turned outward, trained for departure.

Boys were watched closely, expected to remain when their parents grew old.

Ibrahim, my oldest brother, was still small when the adults began teaching him how to stand and listen—hands at his sides, eyes steady. It did not take long before he was sent out alone, his steps quick and certain, no one needing to call after him.

By twelve, Ibrahim was already moving through the streets with Yamma's lists folded small in his pocket, the paper worn soft at the creases, carrying what she could no longer fetch. Yamma had already borne five children—four boys and one girl, Nelly.

By the time I was born, the burden of the household was already his.

Most days, the pot held mujaddarah—lentils and rice pilaf, onions fried until caramelized. Food that stretched as far as it could. Baba, my father's wages were small. Ibrahim's were smaller. Coins reached the table at night, gone by morning. Whatever he earned found its way back into the house.

Yamma lost Fuad, her second son, when he was six.

He was playing in the kitchen when the pot tipped. Boiling water spilled from the burner, struck the stone, and leapt back at him. Steam rose, sudden and blinding.

Then the scream—sharp, unrecognizable.

Days passed. Infection set in. The word gangrene was whispered, then swallowed.

Fuad did not survive.

After that, she remained in the kitchen. She scrubbed the floor until her knuckles split, the tiles worn under her hands. She cooked rigid, eyes fixed ahead, daring nothing to shift.

At night, she pressed her palms into the table long after the food was gone, shoulders locked, her breath held there. She did not cry where anyone could see. A sudden noise made her flinch.

When water boiled, she drew her hands back. Steam made her recoil.

The other children learned to move quietly around her. No one ran in the kitchen or left a pot unattended. The house rearranged itself around what had happened, and nobody said so out loud.

Months passed. Then a year.

The absence had no name anymore—it lived in the walls, in the way she set a pot down, in the pause before she answered when someone called from the other room.

She named her fifth son Fuad, thinking it would ease the pain.

The first time someone called his name across the courtyard, she stilled completely. Just for a moment. Then she kept moving.

It didn't ease anything. But she kept his name alive in the house, and that was the only thing she knew how to do.

Some mornings the house held too much of him. On one of those mornings, she packed a bag and traveled to Jerusalem to visit Khalti Nahme, my aunt.

She passed women selling secondhand clothes outside the Old City walls beneath Damascus Gate, its stone arch rising above the crowd. They laid out dresses, shirts, and children's sweaters across blankets on the hot stone. Vendors shouted prices over one another.

Roasted nuts cracked open. Warm khubz, our daily bread, cooled on metal trays. Sfiha, small flatbreads topped with meat and herbs, pressed tight, baked to a golden brown, steamed beneath thin cloths.

Yamma crouched and sorted, her fingers moving through the piles, reading the seams. She weighed the garments in her palm, testing the hems. Her voice stayed low—a lifted brow, a click of her tongue.

"How much for this?"

"Three liras."

"Three? For this?"

"That's too much."

"Then two."

Yamma slipped the clothing into her bag. When she stood, the bag hung heavy from her arm. The women shook their heads, half amused, half defeated.

Whatever she brought home, she washed in our courtyard, sleeves rolled. She dragged each piece across the ridged tin, scrubbing until the fabric surrendered. The clothes hung along the line, stiff with soap, drying clean.

My family lived in Harat al-Nasarah, the Christian Quarter, where Catholics, Protestants, Orthodox, and Muslim families shared narrow stone lanes that echoed with life and prayers.

Four families shared our building—us on the upper floor, our two rooms opening to the courtyard; Khalti Jamila, my aunt, and Teta, my grandmother Helena, in the neighboring unit, close enough that their footsteps blended with ours; Khalti Suad and her family; and our neighbors below.

Khalti Tamam lived across the street in a room of her own. She spent her days in our home, returning to her room only to sleep.

Doors stayed open. Neighbors passed through without asking. Voices carried across the courtyards, layered with the smell of bread rising in one kitchen and the sound of a baby crying in another, and somewhere always a mother calling her child home in a voice that found its way into the walls and stayed there.

From the alley below, the fruit vendor's call drifted upward.

"Tomatoes, cucumbers, apples."

Greetings floated between balconies.

"Sabah el-khair—good morning, Um Ibrahim," they called, using the title that named her as his mother.

"Sabah el-noor—morning light to you."

When the sun cleared the courtyard wall, the women were already in motion. Tamam's sharp tongue and quick laughter cut through our day.

I stood beside Khalti Tamam, looking up while she held a piece of chocolate between her fingers.

She broke off a bite and brought it to her mouth.

"You want a piece?"

"No. I want the whole thing."

She smiled and took another bite.

"Do you want it now?"

"No. I want the whole thing."

She took another bite, then another, until only a small corner remained. I watched it shrink and waited for the last piece.

That was the end of me wanting the whole thing.

Jamila moved quietly, stepping in where words weren't enough. A scarf was always tied on her head. I never saw her hair down. Not once. She cared for what others forgot—children with fevers, floors swept before dawn, dishes washed and stacked without sound.

When the cold settled deep into the house, I would slip into her bed, pressing against her for warmth. She never pushed me away.

Teta, elderly and steadfast, followed at her own pace, her skin cool against my cheek as she passed. Everything stilled when she entered. She always wore a thob, a long black embroidered dress, and a heta, a hat adorned with small coins that shimmered with each step. Yamma and her sisters saved their thobs for special occasions.

Even the house seemed to bend around her presence. She held her ground in a house that gave way everywhere else.

The roof above us leaked. In winter, rain slipped through the seams and we scrambled to catch it with pots and pans, the metal pinging as water found its mark. Baba never fixed it. There was no money for fixing things—only for managing them.

One room shifted with the day—living space by morning, sleeping quarters by night. Baba's hand-stitched bedding lined the floors. He had made it himself, and you could see where he had pressed the needle through, uneven in places, tight where his patience held and loose where it didn't.

We huddled shoulder to shoulder beneath heavy cotton blankets as cold shot through the stone, the wind nudging the shutters. Nobody complained. Complaining used energy the house couldn't spare.

Our kitchen, no bigger than a walk-in closet, held everything—spices crowding the shelves in sealed jars, mismatched dishes stacked wherever space allowed. A wooden table sat in the corner, its surface scarred from years of kneading, cutting, sorting. Yamma stood at that table every morning. By the time we woke, she had already been there an hour.

Our bathroom was a small shed tucked into the corner of the courtyard, its rigid metal roof rattling, its wooden door barely staying closed. In summer the roof baked. In winter the wind cut through the cracks. During the coldest months, a bucket stayed indoors behind a curtain. Nobody spoke about it. It was simply part of what the house required of you.

Yamma and her sisters wrapped sambousek, small meat-filled pastries, pinching the dough closed, trays filling as stories passed between them. Bread was never wasted. When it molded, we burned it or fed it to the animals.

Most homes had no ovens—only propane burners—so Yamma balanced her tray on her hip, hands dusted with flour, and carried the dough through the hara to the communal bakery. Other women were already there, standing close, waiting their turn, trading news in low voices. The stone oven held ash and heat deep in its walls.

The sound came first—dough meeting heat—then the smell as rounds blistered, freckled where the fire burned hardest.

Water came from the well at the edge of the quarter, women carrying it home on their shoulders, wooden poles across their backs, pails swaying with each step.

Rain never followed a schedule. When the well ran low, we relied on it. After dinner, metal tubs appeared—for dishes, for laundry, sometimes for bathing beneath the open sky.

The muezzin's call to prayer rose over the rooftops—Allahu akbar.

Church bells answered from the far side of the quarter. Ding. Dong.

Nelly, my oldest sister, was fifteen, newly in an arranged union, still learning the rules of another household, when she discovered she was pregnant.

Yamma, in her forties, learned she was pregnant again. "Allah yaster, may God protect us," she said, shielding the life growing inside her. She held to the psalm she knew by heart: children are a gift from the Lord, offspring a reward.

She had borne nine children—seven still moving through the house, one whose absence echoed, and Nelly living a courtyard away. I would be the tenth.

Across the courtyard, Nelly rested a hand on her belly.

"Yamma, we're going to deliver together."

"Inshallah, God willing."

I was woven into their lives before I took my first breath—already an aunt.

Whispers followed.

"Another one?"

"Isn't she too old?"

"How will they manage?"

Yamma heard them—the comments, the quiet judgments that followed her from doorway to doorway. They did not bend her. When voices lowered, she tightened her scarf and kept moving, spine straight.

"Ya Allah, guide me," Yamma prayed silently.

Her marriage to Baba, my father, moved by habit rather than ease. He came home. She put food on the table. They did not touch unless the house required it. There was no softness in it—only rhythm, expectation, survival.

At night, Baba lay awake listening to the house breathe—the rustle of quilts, the scrape of a chair pulled back, the soft clink of a pot set down. The weight of the house pressed in on him, growing heavier with each child.

One night, Ibrahim leaned close to him.

"How are we supposed to manage another?"

Chapter 2

UNEXPECTED SEED

"Before I formed you in the womb, I knew you."
(Jeremiah 1:5, NIV)

Early October stood between the olive harvest and the first rain. Yamma labored in our stone house.

No cries meant for the neighbors. Breath pulled in and out, sweat darkening her scarf, pain rolling through her in waves. Her hands braced against the low table as her body bore down. Tamam stood close at Yamma's side, her hands locked around her, fingers spread with each contraction.

The midwife opened her worn leather satchel on a low, square stool, its seat woven from palm fibers. Inside were folded linen, softened by years of use, a small blade wrapped in cloth, and twine cut to length and set aside. She laid everything down with habitual precision—placing and aligning without looking.

"Water," she said. Boiled, then cooled.

Jamila lifted the pot from the corner and set it within reach. Sheets followed. She pulled the lamp closer, the flame steady, pushing shadows back against the yellowed, cracked walls. The midwife dipped two fingers into the basin and tested the temperature. She lifted her hand, palms up.

Silence. No words—only the signal.

Sunlight slipped through the barred window and settled over Yamma's shoulders, catching the dust as she leaned forward, breath pulled deep, claimed from somewhere older.

On the other side of the wall, in the courtyard, life went on.

A pot shifted on the burner, metal scraping metal. A chicken squawked, sharp and annoyed. In the courtyard, Ibrahim paced the ledge. Each step scraped lightly against the stone. Back and forth, he counted without realizing it.

"Baba," Ibrahim whispered. "Is she going to be okay?"

"Yes. She's stronger than all of us."

His voice didn't rise. The words didn't settle. He kept pacing.

My cry tore through the room and into the courtyard, splitting the hush in two.

The midwife moved fast. Hands sure. The umbilical cord—cut clean. The twine pulled tight. Warm cloths passed over my skin until my color deepened and my breath found its rhythm. She checked my mouth, my fingers, the bend of my feet—touch, pause, touch—her eyes reading my body.

Then she wrapped me and placed me in Ibrahim's arms before anyone else stepped forward.

"Here," she said. "She's yours now."

The midwife turned away. Gathering her things.

Sheets rinsed. Linen folded. The work was done.

My weight startled him—solid, warm, breathing. A spill of pale blond hair brushed his wrist; my eyes blinked open, dark and searching. Ibrahim's breath caught. His shoulders dropped. His hands rested against me.

Baba reached out, brushed my cheek with his thumb, and spoke the name he had carried quietly.

"Hala."

I would not understand until much later what it cost to say a name out loud in this city—to give a child something that could be taken, and give it anyway. That is the only act of faith I have ever fully believed in.

Ibrahim lined my basket with soft linen, attached it to the bicycle, and rode me through Ramallah. The streets were more stone and earth than pavement, worn smooth by feet, carts, and donkeys. Bicycle wheels clicked over rock and dirt beneath us. His hands stayed light on the handles.

The breeze brushed my face. The sway rocked me toward sleep. Shadows passed over the basket—arches, laundry lines, the brief dark of narrow alleys opening and closing above me. I don't remember it. But I have been told it so many times that it lives in my body the way weather does—not recalled, but felt.

I was two when the ground beneath Ramallah began to shift. Work thinned. Coins were counted twice before leaving the house. Conversations started late in the evenings. Possibilities handled like fragile glass. A cousin who knew someone. A sponsor willing to sign. A rumor that the consulate was approving a few visas that month.

Men lined up before dawn outside the consulate doors, papers clutched in damp hands. Their breath clouded the morning air as they waited. Some returned with stamped pages. Others walked back empty-handed, eyes fixed on the ground.

Every step demanded payment—signatures, stamps, photographs, each one heavier than the last. Families like ours scraped together what they could, coin by coin. My aunts slipped off their gold and sold it, piece by piece, to help carry us forward.

"Put this with the rest," Amo Samir, my uncle, said softly. He placed bills into Yamma's hand.

"Take this," Tamam whispered.

Coins and folded liras were stored in a hidden clay pot, its mouth sealed, tucked back into shadow—meant for their journey.

It did not happen all at once. There were papers to gather, names to be written and rewritten, documents folded and checked again. They moved through it quietly, as if too much attention might undo it.

And then it came. Yamma stood still as Ikhwani—my five brothers—kissed her goodbye, her hands trembling at her sides, her face held firm by will alone.

"Take care," Yamma said.

"Allah maakon. God be with you," Baba murmured.

"I'll write often," Ibrahim promised, his voice shaky.

Ikhwani flew to America with only a few coins in their pockets and hope stretched thin. Their absence hollowed out our home. I felt it the way a room feels a missing chair—not in looking for it, but in the new shape of the space.

Soon, the envelopes arrived. Baba opened each one, smoothing the creases before reading aloud. His thumb lingered at the folds—a gesture I watched so many times I came to believe the letter lived twice: once in the words, once in the handling of them.

Voices carried through paper—work found and lost, rooms shared, exhaustion borne without complaint. Names we didn't know yet, streets we couldn't picture, days counted by hours, not seasons. The paper smelled of where it had passed—train smoke, cheap ink, unfamiliar soap. In letters, Ibrahim described the work.

They leaned on relatives—couches, floors shared—until work came. Word passed between men. A door opened. They started by lifting, watching, doing whatever was asked of them.

Rolls of carpet rode their shoulders up narrow stairs, knees burning, skin rubbed raw through thin shirts. Stairwells were tight and airless, thick with dust and old glue.

They stripped rooms down to subfloor—prying, scraping, hauling until nothing remained but boards and breath. Tiles were set piece by piece, mosaic patterns locking together under sore hands.

"I've never seen anyone work so hard," a customer once told them.

"Take a break," his wife suggested. They didn't.

A wide storefront followed, its windows dressed in rolled goods—the kind you noticed before you knew who owned it, its reputation carried in tired bodies.

Dollar bills, crisp, carrying the scent of ink, were

tucked away. The pantry filled first, then the pot.

On better nights, Yamma made makloubeh. Our excitement rose as the pot was lifted, then flipped onto a stainless-steel pan with a shallow lip, releasing the rice, chicken, and vegetables in a mound.

"Yamma... can we have more?" my sister Maha asked.

The pan stood clean.

Their sacrifice opened the gates of the Aziz Shaheen School for Girls. Families dreamed of sending their daughters there. Most never could. The money that arrived in letters made it possible for us to attend. Uniforms were expensive—stiff cotton dresses with green stripes, often patched and handed down, stitched carefully by neighbors who came together to help the girls.

My earliest memories of learning lived in the school courtyard. The sun lit the flagged ground, smoothed by generations of feet. We lined up in stiff cotton uniforms, rows straight as planted seedlings, hands pinned to our sides.

My heart thudded when the teacher called my name.

"Hala."

I stood.

"Next time, speak louder," she said.

I nodded, heat rushing into my face. I did not tell her I had been speaking as loudly as I dared. That is a thing girls learn early in Ramallah: how to calibrate. How to take up exactly as much space as is permitted, and no more.

The days changed without warning.

Men came home quieter. The women moved through the house—brooms scraping stone, pots shifting on burners, water carried, bread torn, work passing from one set of hands to the next.

No one announced lessons. When curfews fractured our school days and the streets emptied early, Baba pulled a notebook closer. He guided my hand slowly, his fingers warm over mine, steady where I shook.

"Slowly," he said. "Let your hand follow the letters."

I pressed the pencil too hard. The tip snapped.

"You did it," he said. "Hada ismuki. That's your name."

Maha took over where he left off, turning Ramallah into a lesson as we walked through town.

"Read this one." She tapped a shop window.

I squinted. "I... I can't."

"You can," she said. "Start with the first sound."

"Good," she whispered.

When we climbed to the rooftop, the noise softened, the street falling away. She lay close enough that her arm brushed mine, her shoulder angled toward me, holding me in place. The stone was warm beneath us. The sky stretched wide above. She named the clouds before I could.

"That one's a horse," she said, her finger cutting through the blue.

"No, it's a sheep," I argued.

She laughed—not to correct me, not to win—then pointed again, slower this time, waiting. I kept looking until I saw what she saw. We believed the clouds were messages meant for us, secrets shared between the sky and our upturned hands. I still look up, sometimes, before I know I'm doing it.

Once, she found me lying belly-down along the stone ledge of our courtyard, my arm dangling over the drop. The air beneath me felt like play, flight waiting its turn.

Maha didn't hesitate. She grabbed my waist and yanked me back, her arms locking around me before fear could reach me. Her heartbeat hammered against my back. She didn't scold me. She held me there, tight and silent, until the shaking stopped—mine and hers.

I have thought about that grip many times since. What it is to love something so fiercely you pull it back from the edge without stopping to think about your own weight.

When Maha was strong, I stayed with her. When she wasn't well—and those days came more often—I drifted toward Frank, my youngest brother.

We built kites from bamboo sticks and scraps of newspaper, sealing them with a flour-and-water paste. They flew until the wind caught them, lifting paper and string into the bright Ramallah sky. We played marbles in a circle and collected stamps, small worlds pressed between our fingers. The alleys of Harat al-Nasarah were our playground. Those afternoons felt endless in the way that only childhood's safe hours do—not because time slowed, but because we had not yet learned to count it.

Spring pushed red poppies through stone and citrus blossoms into the fields. Summer pressed heat into our skin, dust between straps. We hid beneath sycamore trees, their shade falling over us.

Autumn brought long days of gathering, hands

stained and shoulders aching before the light gave out. Winter pulled us inward—lentils simmering low and coal crackling into the night. Chestnuts blistered in the embers, their skins splitting with small pops. The smoke clung to our sleeves as we waited for them to cool in our hands. The house closed tight around its warmth.

During harvest, before dawn, Yamma and Khalti Tamam walked side by side, the rope slack in Yamma's hand as the donkey trailed behind them.

"Yalla, let's go, Hala," Yamma called. "Stay close."

"Stupid donkey," Tamam teased, tugging the rope. "You walk slower than my old bones."

When we reached the trees, we tied the donkey and spread white cloths beneath the branches. Sticks struck the branches. Olives fell in bursts, knocking into one another as leaves broke free. Dust hung in the air. Oil coated our fingers, sharp and green.

"Hala!" Yamma snapped. "Don't eat them raw."

I bit into one anyway. Bitterness twisted my face.

Tamam laughed. "Silly girl, even goats don't make that face."

By afternoon, our sacks were heavy.

"Why so many olives?" I asked.

"Because this is our year," Yamma said. "Some years the trees give plenty. Others, they rest."

The days were long, and the waiting longer.

Mill wheels groaned as they crushed the fruit into paste. Oil ran warm and thick, its scent clinging to our clothes.

"Smell that," Tamam said.

"It smells oily," I said.

"That's because it is," Yamma answered, smiling.

She filled a small tin with the first pressing. We dipped fresh khubz into it, then sprinkled it with zaatar, a thyme-and-sesame blend—sharp, peppery, biting at the back of the tongue. The rest we cured, olives packed into jars, salted and sealed to last.

When winter came and the nights turned cold, Yamma and Khalti Tamam carried the kanun—our coal brazier, a shallow metal basin used for heat—to the bakery at the corner of the hara. They wrapped the sides in cloth so it wouldn't burn them. The baker scraped glowing coals into the basin, selling warmth by the scoop, each ember pulsing orange.

"How much do I owe you?" Yamma asked.

He shook his head. "For Um Ibrahim? Never."

"Kindness doesn't warm a home," she said.

"Maybe not," he replied. "These black diamonds will."

"Allah ybarek fik. God bless you," Yamma said.

Peace carried us through those seasons—until soldiers flooded Ramallah again.

Boots struck the stone of our hara hard and fast. Doors slammed open along the street. Metal rang against metal. Each door they kicked open brought them closer.

When they reached our building, the wooden door below shuddered. The window grates rattled.

Baba pulled Frank close. Yamma swept her arm around Maha and me, guiding us behind the kanun. The coals glowed low.

"Baba," Frank whispered. "Are they coming in?"

"Stay still," Baba said. "Don't make any noise."

My heart beat so hard I pressed my lips together. Maha's fingers slid into mine, slick with sweat.

Outside, shouts rose—sharp, mocking.

"Still hiding?"

"Come out. See how free you are."

I listened for the latch to give. The wood to split. The night to spill in.

We heard the metal click of rifles. Light slipped through the grates. A match had been struck outside.

"They're rats," someone said. "Afraid of daylight."

When the footsteps finally moved on, Yamma loosened her grip. Air returned. Somewhere down the alley, another door slammed, and my body flinched before my mind caught up. That is the thing about fear—it gets into your muscles. Long after the sound ends, your body goes on listening.

Days passed before the street felt whole again.

Yamma finally walked me into the city. She kept her hand firm at my wrist—not guiding so much as anchoring me. Her grip didn't ease when I stumbled. I stayed close to the places she trusted, steps she had taken a thousand times, routes her body knew.

El-Manara opened wide before us.

The servees—taxis—idled at the curb, engines low and constant, heat rising off the metal. Horns cut through the air—sharp, impatient, never alone. Drivers called out destinations into the noise. Children slipped through the crowd, quick and fearless, brushing past without looking. The buses came and went without announcement—and in our hands, paper tickets—creased, numbered, passed from palm to palm—small proofs that we were part of it, already in motion.

At the center, the stone lions stood, worn smooth by hands and weather, their faces dulled but unmoved. I reached out and touched one. The stone was cool beneath my palm.

"Hala," Yamma said.

She rested her hand over mine, her fingers firm.

"These lions have watched wars pass, mourners gather, wedding dances rise, footsteps fade, and children grow old."

"They don't forget."

I held that with me. I still hold it. There is a difference, I have learned, between endurance and stubbornness. The lions were not stubborn. They simply stayed. And staying, in a place that gives you every reason to leave, is its own form of faith.

Our home was small and worn. It was enough. A roof that sheltered less than it leaked. Water gifted from the sky. Heat gathered from embers, warmth stitched into Baba's quilts. Bread stretched across days, olive oil and za'atar shared at the table, coins counted quietly before they were spent. In our home, we found peace.

Then a letter arrived.

Baba opened it at the table, running his hand over the paper before unfolding it. I watched his face the way children watch weather—not understanding the pressure systems, only reading what they mean for the day ahead.

"They're working hard," he said. "And they miss us."

The kanun burned low in the corner. Cold pressed in from the walls. Maha leaned forward, elbows on the table. Baba looked at the page again, longer this time.

He folded the letter carefully.

Then again.

Outside, the street was quiet. Inside, we all understood that something had shifted—not broken, not decided, but tilted, the way a scale tilts before you've finished adding weight. We did not speak of it that night. We did not need to. Some conversations happen entirely in the folding of paper, in the sound of a man going still.

I was young. But I knew, the way children always know before they have the words for it: we were going to leave. And leaving would not be the end of us.

It would be the next thing we survived.

Chapter 3

THE HARVEST

"To everything there is a season,
a time to weep and a time to laugh,
a time to mourn and a time to dance."
(Ecclesiastes 3:1, 4, NIV)

The man who came back wasn't the one who left. I hid behind Yamma's red dress. My fingers hooked into the fabric at her calf.

He stood in the doorway.

Drums threaded through the streets of Harat al-Nasarah, bouncing off limestone walls. From the street below, two women called to each other.

"Ya Um Samir, did you hear the drumming today?"

"Aywa, yes, the youth are practicing again."

"For what?"

"For what's coming."

Their voices reached our windows, blending with the drums. The hara moved. Sounds carried.

Yamma's hands moved to the worn corner of the tablecloth—the fabric thinned from years of folding. She opened the wooden drawer of photographs. She lifted one picture, its corners soft and bent. The face in the picture was a boy's, smiling. She held it. Her voice wavered, her mouth opening, then closing.

"I can't... I can't talk about them anymore."

The words came out thin and stopped.

Baba didn't rush to fix it. He sat there with his tea cooling, the steam thinning into nothing, staring at the surface. His jaw tightened, then loosened, his fingers relaxing around the cup. I had seen him do that before—hold something until the shape of holding it changed. That is what grief looked like in our house: not crying, but going very still.

Outside, falafel sizzled in hot oil. Pastries rested on wooden boards near open windows, butter and sugar drifting into the streets.

Under a tin roof that held the heat, the coffee shop gathered the fathers and grandfathers—the smell of coffee rising between them, cups clinking, dice knocking on wood, cards laid down in games like gin rummy, smoke curling above backgammon boards. Men called to each other across the tables, voices tossed and caught.

In courtyards and each other's homes, coffee cooled in small cups. When they finished, the women turned them over, waiting for the coffee grounds to settle, tracing shapes along the porcelain—part storytelling, part fortune, part connection. I believed in those readings then. I believed the future had already been poured, and the women were simply learning to see it.

By late morning, the postman passed through the hara, letters tucked under his arm. One for us. Baba's hands trembled as he opened it at the table.

Ibrahim wrote that he was coming home to marry.

The news spread through Ramallah. Our house woke all at once. Pillows were fluffed. Cups were rinsed twice.

Weeks went by before we heard from Ibrahim again. Back then, no homes had phones. Our only connection was a phone at Abu Jereious's coffee shop on the corner. The coffee shop owner's son came running, out of breath. He carried news for the whole hara. He carried ours.

"Ibrahim called from Tel Aviv. He'll be here soon."

By the time the message reached our door, Ibrahim was in Ramallah.

"Zaghareet!"

"Zaghareet."

Khalti Tamam shouted, her hands lifted high. A sharp trill—rolling from the tongue—pierced the courtyard.

Yamma smoothed the pillows, her eyes darting to the door, fixed there. Baba lingered at the doorway longer than usual, scanning the alley, shoulders tense.

Footsteps echoed in our courtyard, louder and closer than the others, and my stomach flipped. Yamma froze, her hand stopping in mid-air.

"Huwwa, is it him?"

"Aywa, huwa. Yes, it's him."

Baba said it quietly, not trusting his voice.

His absence had lived in the house instead—in Yamma's sigh when his name was mentioned, in the way Baba went quiet, in photographs handled until the corners wore thin. Absence in our house had its own weight, its own chair at the table, its own silence at meals. And now the absence was walking toward us.

"Ya ibni, ya habibi, my son, my love."

Her voice broke into tears as she moved toward him, the words rushing ahead of her body.

"Ishtaqnalak ktir, we missed you so much."

Ibrahim kissed her cheeks, one side then the other.

"Ana kaman ishtaqtillik, I missed you too," he said.

Baba cleared his throat. His smile brightened, though he tried to stay calm, his chin lifting.

"Welcome back, ya ibni, my son."

"The house hasn't felt the same without you."

I peeked out from behind Yamma's arm, fingers twisting the hem of my dress until the fabric rolled tight. He stood before me as both kin and stranger—known through photographs, not through memory. That is a particular kind of loneliness: to love someone you cannot quite place.

He crouched to my level.

"Hala..."

I didn't answer.

"It's me," he said softly. "I'm your big brother."

His smile flickered.

"Wow... you're prettier than I remember."

Yamma nudged me, gentle but firm.

"Hadha akhi—this is your brother."

The boy in the pictures stood in front of me, shaped by years I didn't have. I looked at the floor, at the crack in the stone where dust gathered.

"Yamma, I'm scared," I said, tugging her sleeve.

She lifted my chin with her fingertips, her thumb warm under my jaw, steady where I wasn't.

"Don't be scared, habibti, my love."

"Yalla, go."

Ibrahim opened his arms, not reaching—waiting.

"Hala, taali—come here."

"I missed you."

I took one step, then another, and then my feet decided for me. He held me tight without squeezing me.

"You grew," he laughed.

"You left," I whispered.

He went still for just a moment. Not a long moment. But I felt it—the way you feel a room change temperature before you understand why. He had no answer for that. There isn't one. And even then, at that age, some part of me knew it: I wasn't accusing him. I was just naming what was true. You grew. You left. Both things. At once.

He held me, then set me down gently.

My hands kept twisting the hem of my dress.

The air shifted before I could settle.

An American woman stepped into our Ramallah doorway.

"Hadi khatibti, this is my fiancée," Ibrahim said.

The room went the way rooms go when something unexpected enters them—not loud, not rude, just slightly slower. A breath held half a second too long.

In our family, women came forward—arms open, cheeks offered, bodies moving before words. You did not wait. You moved. That was love. That was how we recognized each other.

Yamma didn't cross the room. She stayed where she was and smiled the smile she used with officials—correct, complete, and closed as a locked drawer.

"Ahlan wa sahlan," she said. Welcome. The word was right. The warmth behind it was somewhere else.

I waited for her to open her arms the way she always did. She didn't.

The woman stayed planted near the doorway, her body tight, one hand around her bag strap. Her eyes moved across the room—the low table, the crowded chairs, the faces arranged in welcome that was not quite welcome.

Khalti Tamam, who had never in her life met a woman she didn't immediately claim as her own, found something to straighten on the table. Her hands moved over the cloth, smoothing creases that were not there. She did not look up.

Khalti Jamila stepped forward with coffee—that much, at least, was offered. The woman smiled and nodded, but did not reach for the cup. She spoke in English. Jamila set the cup down without filling the silence that followed.

Relatives poured in from Jerusalem. Our one room crowded with bodies. They greeted Ibrahim with both hands, with exclamations, with the names of his childhood. They greeted her with nods. In our family, a nod was what you gave a stranger at the market. It was not nothing. It was not enough.

If an aunt stepped closer, she shifted back.

If an uncle laughed, she did not.

If a friend reached for me, she watched, but her hand never followed.

Baba's welcome came formal—the kind of welcome you give at a gate, not a woman entering the family. His eyes found Ibrahim's and stayed there, asking a question he would never ask out loud.

Ibrahim answered it by not answering it. He kept his hand on her back and his smile fixed and his eyes moving, room to room, person to person, translating everything into a language neither side fully spoke.

I watched it all from behind Yamma's arm. I did not have the words for what I was seeing. I only knew that the room felt like a table set for a meal where someone had quietly removed a chair, and everyone could see the empty space, and no one was going to say so.

She was far from home. That much I understood. What I did not understand yet was that you can be far from home and also be in the wrong one.

Two weeks later, Ibrahim and I were inseparable—this time in a car, not on his bicycle.

Every time I slid into the seat beside him, his shoulders rose before he spoke, adjusting the mirror, his shirt—anything but me.

She muttered in English from the front seat, her eyes sliding past me to the window.

"Is she coming with us?"

The question landed the way it was meant to—quietly, so it could be denied later. I did not understand the English. But I understood the tone. Children always understand the tone.

Ibrahim's hand landed on my shoulder and stayed.

"Always."

He said it without looking at her. He said it the way our family said things that were not up for discussion—not loud, not hard, just settled. Final as a door closing.

He jingled his keys and looked down at me. We shared a small smile.

"Yalla, Hala. Let's ride through town."

We drove with the windows down, Ramallah pouring in—people waving, children laughing, horns blaring, voices weaving together.

Once, he had pedaled me through these same streets with me tucked into a basket. Now I sat beside him, carried differently—feet on the floor. I thought about that without knowing I was thinking about it: how the same person can carry you in entirely different ways, and you are still, in both cases, carried.

"When Yamma was pregnant with you, I was scared."

I frowned. "Why were you scared? I wasn't doing anything."

He let out a small laugh.

"When I first held you, I loved you in a way I didn't expect. I missed you. I just wanted to hold you again."

I smiled and leaned closer. Outside, Ramallah kept moving. I pressed my shoulder against his arm and let the city blur past the window. Some things don't need answering.

Before the wedding, everything was as it had always been—careful, contained, held in place.

Ibrahim's celebration lasted five days—music, laughter, joy that pressed against the skin until it hurt. It spilled past our courtyard walls, pulling the entire hara into its orbit.

Lanterns glowed above the crowd, gold catching on

faces lifted in song. Dabke stomped the earth awake—palms linked, shoulders tight, the line moving as one body. The tabla drum pounded like a second heartbeat.

Men who had known Ibrahim since childhood nodded as they passed, hands over their hearts. Elders stayed longer than usual. His name spread from person to person.

Ibrahim bent down, grinning.

"Hala! Come on—let's see how well you can move."

I planted my fists on my hips. "Oh, you think I can't dance?"

Maha burst into laughter. "Show him, Hala!"

I leapt into the line—my feet stumbling at first, then catching the rhythm. Maha grabbed my hand and yanked me forward, pulling me into the moment.

Around us, the bride and groom were lifted high on chairs, carried above the crowd—music rising, voices singing, hands clapping in time.

My ankles caught the step, my lungs kept up, my fear slipped off for a few beats when the tabla hit hard enough to drown everything else out.

"Wow, Hala—you're doing great!"

"I told you I could!"

Then, in the middle of all that joy, a cold note slipped in—not enough to stop me, enough to blur.

She was standing at the edge of the courtyard. Not dancing. Not quite watching. Her arms crossed low, not in anger—in the posture of someone who does not know where to put their hands when everyone around them knows exactly what their hands are for.

The aunts moved past her like water around a stone.

Not cruelty—nothing so deliberate. They simply flowed where the warmth was, and she was not it. No one pulled her in. No one pressed a plate into her hands or showed her how to hold the dabke line. In our family, those were the acts of love. Their absence was its own answer.

Ibrahim caught my eye from across the line. Something moved in his face—quick, then gone. He smiled at me. I smiled back. We both looked away from her at the same moment, and I have never forgotten that. How easy it was to look away. How we all did it.

The tabla hit again. I kept dancing. But I felt it there—that edge—the way you feel the cold side of a room even when you're standing in the warm part.

Small plates covered the table—hummus glossed with olive oil, baba ghanoush smoky, labneh drizzled, olives brined, pickled vegetables bright, falafel crisp, stuffed grape leaves, warm bread torn by hand.

Desserts followed—kanafeh, syrup clinging to melting cheese, ma'amoul dusted in sugar that clung to our fingers and lips.

"Hala, leave some for the guests!"

Yamma called across the table.

I looked up, my mouth full, and Maha laughed, already reaching for another piece.

Later, as the music deepened, a belly dancer moved into the center, her body answering a rhythm we all knew. Shisha pipes released apple-scented smoke, the charcoal glowing low as it drifted between us. Men leaned forward, conversation softening around her.

"She doesn't just dance," a man breathed, a shisha pipe hanging loose from his hand.

"She becomes the rhythm."

The women, glowing in black thobs embroidered with red, the stitching bright against the dark cloth, moved around the bride—adjusting her veil, murmuring blessings, hands quick and gentle. The scent of henna rose, fresh and earthy, as we decorated our hands, the stains deepening as they settled into our skin.

"Don't move." Maha said it without looking up.

"I'm not!"

"You're moving."

"I'm breathing!"

The night before the ceremony, we prepared the sashes—mashlahat, almonds, and chocolates wrapped in silk—for the guests, stacking them one beside the other.

On the morning itself, Maha and I were flower girls in white, our sandals slipping, our bouquets fragrant in our hands as we stood near the church entrance. Beside us, the mashlahat were placed within reach. As guests arrived, they were greeted and handed their sashes, each one received with a nod, a blessing, a name spoken aloud.

Friends, family, and neighbors filled the church courtyard, pressing in to offer their congratulations, voices overlapping until the air felt thick with blessing.

After the ceremony, a lamb was slaughtered before the doorway. The bride and groom stepped over it, their hands marked with blood pressed against the walls for blessing. The lamb turned slowly over charcoal, the fire catching and darkening the skin. Later, it was carved and passed among family and close friends.

Ibrahim stayed two months—long enough for the rooms to feel full again, long enough for me to start believing it could stay that way. That is the cruelty of a visit: it teaches your body what it has been missing. Then it ends, and your body has to learn the absence all over again, this time knowing exactly what it is.

Before he left, he told my parents he had begun the paperwork to bring us to America. Forms, stamps, signatures—none of it meant anything to me. Paper was paper. Ibrahim was Ibrahim. I did not yet understand that paper could move mountains, or that it could also refuse to.

One morning, Yamma folded clothes, lining edges that didn't need lining, and Baba kept checking the doorway.

"Are you going back?" I asked.

He paused.

"Yes—so I can bring you to me."

"You promise?"

"I promise."

As he walked toward the door, I wrapped myself around his leg, gasping between sobs, my face against the fabric of his pants, my hands gripping.

"Please don't go."

"Please."

Baba rested a hand on my shoulder, unmoving. I didn't look at him. If I did, I might let go.

Ibrahim kept walking. That is the thing I have never forgotten—not as cruelty, but as necessity. He had to keep walking or he would not be able to walk at all. I understand it now. Then, I only felt the leg moving under my arms, and my hands losing their grip, and the space where he had been filling with nothing.

Maha pulled me in, her arm around my shoulders. Her breath against my hair. I pressed my face into her sweater and stayed there, listening until my breathing matched hers.

I didn't understand why he was leaving.

Only Maha's arms around me.

Morning came slowly. Evenings lingered.

Ibrahim flew to America; restrictions returned, unwelcome, over Ramallah like a lid. Streets emptied earlier. Voices lowered. Doors closed sooner than they used to.

Maha's breathing changed. I noticed it in the way she stopped mid-sentence. Her breaths thinned. The pauses stretched.

"Breathe slowly."

Yamma's hand hovered near Maha's back.

"I'm here."

I watched Yamma's hand. How it didn't touch, not yet—just hovered, close enough that Maha could feel the warmth of it. That is its own kind of language. The almost-touch. The hand that says: I am here, right here, whenever you need me to land.

The journey to America began in Jerusalem, with paperwork stacked higher than the table.

Offices were jammed with families. Lines snaked through hallways, shoulders close together, eyes ahead. The air smelled of ink, nerves, and sweat.

"Next," the clerk called.

Baba stepped forward, the papers in both hands.

"Your daughter's medical report is incomplete."

"Which daughter?"

"It doesn't specify."

"Come back tomorrow."

Screenings followed—rooms sharp with the smell of chlorine and worry. Cold chairs. Harsh lights. Numbers called. Names bent out of shape. People whispering. I learned something in those rooms: that a family can be reduced to a stack of papers, and a stack of papers can be told to come back tomorrow, and tomorrow is not a promise. Tomorrow is just another word for waiting.

At home, Ramallah kept breathing.

Khalti Tamam crossed the courtyard carrying khubz from the bakery. Teta's footsteps dragged softly across stone. Nelly's voice floated through an open window. The city did not loosen its hold.

"What if they refuse Maha?"

Yamma asked one night when the lamps burned low, shadows trembling against the walls.

"We trust God," Baba said.

His hand tightened around his coffee, the liquid sloshing and never spilling. I watched that too—the cup that did not spill. All those years of holding things carefully. All those years of not letting anything fall.

One late morning, Baba opened a thin envelope from the consulate at the kitchen table.

He stopped mid-motion.

"It's done," he said.

The room shifted. I stood still. Outside, a drum sounded somewhere in the hara — distant, then gone.

The letter said one word: approved. This, I understood now. This was what was coming. Not an ending. A door, finally, swinging open on the other side of all that waiting.

A red stamp stared from the page—final.

Chapter 4

COMPACTED SOIL

"The light shines in the darkness,
and the darkness has not overcome it."
(John 1:5, NIV)

The notices returned. "Yalla, inside," Yamma said.

Maha and I stayed close.

The loudspeaker boomed across Ramallah.

"All residents: curfew begins immediately."

"No movement outside your homes."

Entrances slammed shut along our hara. The rooms went quiet.

Maha's breath hitched.

"Hala..." she breathed, eyes on the shaking door.

"I'm here," I answered, leaning closer.

The light flickered. Boots scraped the outside stone—one step, then another. The blow struck our metal door—the frame shuddered—bang. Maha's hand gripped mine as Yamma pulled us into her arms. Another blow rattled the windows.

"Open!" a soldier shouted.

The door shook under his fist.

I stopped breathing—and didn't know when to start again.

Maha's fingers dug into mine as the boots circled—closer, then right outside.

Her thumb moved once against my hand—back and forth, like checking I was still there.

I pressed back. That was all I had. I pressed back.

I waited for the door to split open.

It didn't.

Not that time.

The ringing came first—thin and sharp, like something left inside my ear. When I tried to pull my hand away, Maha's fingers stayed locked around mine. Half-moons marked my skin where her nails had pressed.

Dust drifted from the top of the doorframe, settling onto Yamma's sleeve.

None of us brushed it off.

"This house," a soldier said, his voice dropping.

We didn't move.

The footsteps shifted to the neighbor's door, then farther down the street.

Yamma exhaled.

I tried to unclench my fingers.

They wouldn't open.

By morning, the city looked different—streets empty, notices fluttering, people lifting their shutters an inch to peek out.

Yamma scanned the alley, her scarf pulled tight.

"Don't step past the line," she said, pointing to the red mark across the stone.

"Not even one foot."

Across the alley, someone had tried to scrub it. A pale smear stretched over the red, but it bled through again.

A boy from the next building lifted his foot, testing it—his mother yanked him back so fast his sandal scraped loose and skidded across the line.

The air felt different above it. As if stepping there would make a sound even if I didn't move.

I lifted my heel, hovering it above the line. I don't know how long I stood like that. Long enough to understand what a line is for—not to mark where you cannot go, but to mark what they think you are. Something to be kept. Something to be contained. I put my heel down on my side. I did not feel safe. But I felt something else: that I was still the one deciding where my foot landed.

Some mornings, the school gates were locked. Other days, teachers rushed us.

"Hurry," one urged, glancing toward the road. "We don't know how long we have."

Roll call felt different.

A girl stood at the front, reciting. She missed a word.

No one laughed.

The teacher corrected her too quickly, chalk snapping against the board. Dust fell in a soft line beneath it.

We all sat straighter than usual.

"Hala?" the teacher called.

"Hona—here," I said, raising my hand. My fingers stayed half-raised a moment, like they hadn't heard me stop. I lifted it too high, then dropped it fast. Even my body had learned to be uncertain about how much space it was allowed to take.

One day, in the middle of recess—mint still on my fingers from the labneh sandwich Yamma packed—the loudspeaker crackled.

"Students, return home immediately."

"Curfew in effect."

The yard emptied, books clutched, braids flying. Maha grabbed my wrist.

"Don't let go."

She used to say it laughing, pulling me too fast around corners.

Now her fingers tightened as she meant it.

Our hands slipped once. Then found each other again.

A shopkeeper dragged his metal shutter halfway down, then stopped to watch us pass. A single shoe lay in the middle of the road, turned on its side. I looked at it as we ran past and thought: someone left in a hurry. Someone left without their shoe. I did not look back to see if it was still there.

The jeep came as a sound first—low and heavy, before it turned into shape at the end of the lane. She pulled me close. We walked the narrow lanes, each step quickening as the rumble grew, dust lifting around our ankles.

When school stopped, Baba taught us at home.

He handed us books. "Read quietly."

He sat at the table, flour dusting his sleeves. "Let's

read a little before dark."

Flour clung to his fingers, leaving pale prints along the page when he turned it. He paused once, head tilted toward the door. His hand stayed on the page a second too long. Then he nodded for me to continue. My voice trembled as I traced the letters.

"Slowly."

He guided my finger along the line.

"You'll get there."

He said it about the reading. I understood, even then, that he meant more than the reading.

Our hara went dark.

Baba set the book aside.

"Enough," he said quietly.

Yamma lit a single candle.

The room contracted around the flame—our faces drawn in, the walls pushed back into shadow, everything outside that small circle of light made distant and uncertain. We became, for a moment, only what the candle could see: Yamma's hands. Baba's sleeve. Maha's face, tipped slightly toward the warmth.

"One flame is enough," Yamma said. "God sees it."

I have thought about that sentence many times since. Not as comfort—though it was comfort. As instruction. One flame. Hold it steady. That is sufficient. That is, in fact, everything.

Wax gathered at the base, hardening in uneven ridges. Somewhere nearby, a chair scraped. We all heard it.

The flame bent when a door slammed far down the street, then steadied. Yamma cupped her hand around it.

We sat close, listening for footsteps, for doors, for anything that would tell us where the night was moving.

Jamila slipped through our door.

"Close the curtain."

From beneath her shawl, she pulled out a small radio and began to crank it. Static hissed—sharp and restless.

Maha leaned closer.

"Maybe it's scared too," she said.

No one answered. No one laughed. We just sat with it—the idea that fear could live inside a machine, that even a radio could be uncertain about what it was receiving. Maha had a way of saying true things sideways, so they could enter without resistance. I did not know then how few years I had left to collect them.

The static stayed.

We listened anyway.

As shutters shook from distant boots, the women gathered.

Some leaned against the walls. Others sat on the cold steps, skirts spreading, knees touching. One carried thread. Another a dress to mend.

"Did you hear?"

"Hear what?"

Soft laughter moved through them.

"Damascus Gate closed again."

"For what reason?"

"For the same reason as always... none."

They went back to stitching.

"They may silence our voices, not our hands,"

Yamma said.

I watched their hands move in the low light—needle through cloth, thread pulled taut, a knot tied and bitten clean. Creating. In the middle of all that erasure, they were creating. I filed that away somewhere I didn't know I had yet. The place where you keep the things that will hold you up later.

When Yamma finished my small thob—mountains across the front, olive branches along the sleeves—she draped it over my lap and smoothed it once.

"There she is," she said.

Maha watched from the corner.

The yarn slid from her lap without her noticing. Her hook rested in her hand, unmoving.

I nudged the yarn back toward her foot. She didn't pick it up. I looked at her hands—the same hands that had gripped mine through the door, that had found me in the school yard, that had held me on the rooftop. They were still. I did not know what to do with stillness in Maha. Maha was not still. Maha was the one who moved. I picked up the yarn myself and held it, because I did not know what else to do. Because holding a thing is sometimes the only answer to watching it slip.

She had been thinning.

Her sleeves slipped down her arms when she lifted them, like they no longer belonged to her. Her voice arrived a half-second later than usual, as though it had farther to travel. At meals, she ate slowly, carefully, like someone rationing something that couldn't be replaced.

"Yamma..." she said one evening, pressing her hand to her chest.

"It hurts."

She didn't finish the breath that followed. It caught halfway.

I kept breathing, so there would still be one of us.

Yamma pressed her palm to Maha's forehead, her eyes doing the thing they did when she was calculating—not panicking, calculating. What she had. What she needed. What could be done before morning.

"Slow breaths, habibti."

I watched Maha try. I counted her breaths without meaning to. I have always counted things when I am afraid. It gives the fear somewhere to go.

Curfew tightened.

Some days, the streets opened for an hour.

"Yalla! Move!" a soldier shouted.

Once, a soldier stopped Baba.

"Where is your permit?"

Baba held it out. The soldier took it and held it too long—not reading, just holding. Then he let it fall. The paper fluttered once before landing face-down in the dust. The soldier's boot landed beside it, close enough that the edge of the sole touched the corner of the page.

Baba waited. One breath. Two. The kind of waiting that is not patience but discipline—the kind that costs something every time.

Then he bent. Slowly, without hurry, as if the choice to move were entirely his own. He lifted the paper. He brushed it clean with two fingers, the same way he brushed flour from a page. He folded it once and placed it in his pocket.

He said nothing.

That was the bravest thing I ever saw him do. Not the bending. The saying nothing. The keeping of his face. The walking away as if he were the one who had decided when it was over.

At school, warning shots cracked outside the gates.

"Don't make a sound," the teacher said.

We froze.

On a rare break, children burst into the street.

"Hala!" a woman called. "Run while you can—before they lock us in again!"

That night, Yamma tucked the blanket beneath my chin.

"Sleep. Tomorrow will come."

"What if they come back?" I asked.

"They come," she said. "And they go."

She said it the same way every time. Not as reassurance. As fact. They come. And they go. We are the ones who remain.

A letter arrived from Ibrahim. Baba read it aloud.

"Start the papers—I'm ready to bring you here."

At the consulate, the clerk flipped through the documents without looking up.

"Your daughter's medical report is incomplete."

"Which daughter?" Baba asked.

"Come back tomorrow."

A fan turned slowly overhead, clicking at each rotation. The papers stayed perfectly stacked. The clerk had already moved on. Baba had not. He stood for a moment with his hands at his sides, the way he had stood after the permit, after every small erasure—recollecting himself from the inside out, making himself whole again before turning to walk back through the door.

"What if they refuse Maha?" Yamma asked one night.

"We trust God," Baba said.

The street outside filled faster than usual. Doors pulled inward one by one. It didn't empty all at once. It drained.

The letter came in time.

"It's done," Baba said.

He set the envelope on the table and did not pick it up again. Some news you read once and then leave where it is, because you need a moment before it becomes real.

Leaving Ramallah meant goodbye to Teta, my grandmother, and Khalati, my aunts, along with the friends and neighbors who had held our lives.

"Hala, remember your roots," Teta said, her hands shaking as she cupped my face.

I walked through the house, touching everything—the stone walls, the window where bells and Adhan braided, the kanun, the ledge where Maha saved me. Each room was the same as it had always been. That was the hardest part. Nothing had changed except that I was about to.

At the door, I stopped.

My hand rested against the metal—the same place it had shaken under the blows.

It was still now. Cool. Unmoving.

Behind me, no one reached for it.

For a moment, I thought—if I stay, it will all stay. The door. The line. Maha's hand in mine.

I waited—just long enough to feel that it wasn't true.

I looked down at my hand—half-expecting the half-moons to still be there.

They weren't.

But I curled my fingers anyway.

Then I let go.

We left anyway.

Chapter 5

UPROOTED

"When you pass through the waters, I will be with you;
and when you pass through the rivers,
they will not sweep over you."
(Isaiah 43:2, NIV)

Not arriving—departing. I was eight when I left, with Frank ten and Maha twelve, the three of us clustered around Yamma and Baba.

The terminal hummed—announcements echoing overhead, suitcases thudding onto carts, leather handles creaking as people lifted them. The scent of baked khubz, strong coffee, and zaatar drifted as people passed. I breathed it in without knowing I was memorizing it. The body does that—stores what the mind hasn't yet decided to keep.

"Final boarding for Flight 246 to New York."

I held Yamma's hand, my fingers tracing the roughness of her skin. She didn't let go. I tilted my face toward hers.

"Yamma... how far is America?"

She didn't answer right away. Her gaze shifted to the terminal windows, where planes waited.

“Far enough to start again,” she said. “Not far enough to forget.”

The departure hall lights flickered overhead, washing everything in a yellow glow—rows of red vinyl seats, families huddled close, strangers holding passports, papers tucked carefully inside. I watched Yamma thumb the strap of her purse, her jaw set as she scanned the room. She was reading it the way she read every room—finding the exits, the dangers, the faces that would look back.

When the gate agent called us forward, my stomach growled. We walked across the open tarmac, heat lifting off the ground in waves. The plane loomed ahead, loud and breathing.

Metal stairs waited at its base. I tightened my grip on Yamma’s hand as we climbed. The wind tugged at my dress. The engines roared close enough to rattle the air. With each step, the ground fell farther away.

“Yamma… will we come back?”

She kissed my forehead, her lips lingering longer than usual.

“Home goes where we go, ya qalbi, sweetheart.”

I didn’t know then what that sentence would cost her to believe. I only held it. Pressed it into my chest like something I might need later.

On the Alitalia plane, rows of crimson seats stretched endlessly. The air was cool, my cheek against the window.

“It looks beautiful up here,” I said.

Maha leaned beside me, her breath fogging the glass.

"Everything looks so small."

The engines thundered beneath my feet. My heart kept time with them. The land slipped away, shrinking until the olive groves, the limestone homes, and winding alleys of Ramallah blurred into a patchwork of color—greens and tans and the pale gold of stone—until there was nothing left to distinguish one thing from another. Until it was just earth. Until it was just distance.

"Yamma... will there be curfews there too?"

She rested her palm on my head.

"No, sweet girl. Not like here."

A stewardess with kind eyes stopped beside me. She bent down, her smile soft, and placed a cardboard box in my lap. In accented Arabic, she said,

"Hadi ilik, these are for you."

"Ursumi eshi jamīlan." Draw something beautiful.

I looked down at the box, unsure if I was meant to open it. My fingers rested on the lid before lifting it. Inside were brightly colored crayons, a small stack of white paper, the pages clean and waiting. A piece of chocolate lay beside them.

In Ramallah, toys were made from scraps—marbles rescued from dust, dolls shaped from popsicle sticks, kites held together with flour paste, notebooks shared until the paper thinned. I had never been given something new simply because I was there. Simply because I was a child on a plane who might want to draw.

I folded my hands in my lap.

"God, thank you. Please be with us."

The wings vibrated beneath the hum of whispered conversations. I watched the stewardesses, the way they moved with ease through the narrow aisle—unhurried, certain. I looked at Yamma, whose silence spoke more than words—the worry, the exhaustion etched into the curve of her spine. She was holding something together that no one could see.

Baba didn't turn from the television—the single screen at the front, the film translated into Arabic. Frank sat quietly beside him, knees pulled in.

I opened the box and chose a crayon. Blue. The color of the sky outside the window—the same sky over Ramallah, I told myself. The same one. I pressed it to the page and drew the only thing I knew how to draw from memory: our house. The stone walls. The barred window. The courtyard where Maha had pulled me back from the ledge. I drew it small, in the corner of the page, and left the rest white.

Twelve hours later, John F. Kennedy International Airport swallowed us.

I had expected more sky. Instead, there were ceilings—high and vast and lit from above, but ceilings. Light flashed off polished floors that reflected our feet back at us as we walked, doubling us, making a second family that moved in perfect silence beneath the first. People surged in waves—faces from every corner of the world, voices layered in languages I couldn't understand. Moving staircases carried people upward and out of sight. I stopped in front of one and watched a woman step onto it without breaking her stride, without looking down, without holding anything.

“Everything moves fast here,” I said, gripping Yamma’s hand.

“Then we learn to walk faster.”

I sped up like a startled chicken.

“Ikhwani!” Maha gasped. “They’re right there!”

At the bottom of the moving stairs stood Ikhwani.

“They don’t look like the pictures,” I said.

“Neither do we,” Maha said, smoothing her dress. “We’re still family.”

Jimmy stepped forward, pulling Frankie closer.

“You grew so much.”

“Not enough,” Frank said, straightening, a shy smile crossing his face.

I stood slightly behind Maha and watched them—these men who were my brothers, who existed in my life as photographs and envelope handwriting and the sound of Yamma crying quietly after reading their letters. They were taller than I had imagined. Their hands were rough. They smelled of a place I didn’t know yet.

They were real. That was the strangest thing. After all that distance, after all that paper—they were simply real.

Outside, yellow cars with writing on their sides blared their horns. People hurried past us on the sidewalks.

Beneath our feet, something rumbled—a low shaking that moved through the ground and into the soles of my shoes and up through my legs. In Ramallah, the ground shook when soldiers came. Here it was only the subway, Ibrahim said. I did not know yet how to teach my body the difference.

Buildings soared high enough to swallow the sky. I leaned toward the car window. Lights and signs, large boards towering above the street, blurred past.

"Is it always this fast?" I asked.

Ibrahim caught my eye in the rearview mirror.

"It never stops, Hala. You learn to keep up."

Ramallah moved with rhythm—vendors calling out prices, children racing through alleys, neighbors shouting greetings from open windows. Everything had a reason for its sound. Here, everything sounded different. Cars rushed without pause. Sirens cut through. No voices lingered. No one slowed.

We drove on until the noise thinned, until steel and glass gave way to trees and quieter streets. Houses appeared—lighter, narrower, built from wood instead of stone. I pressed my hand to the window.

Westervelt Avenue. North Plainfield. A yellow duplex with chipped paint stood at the curb, quiet and patient, as if it had been waiting.

"This is it," Ibrahim said.

"Simple," he added. "And it's ours."

We moved through it slowly. Four bedrooms opened one by one, each with its own door, its own corners. A dining room waited, its table bare. The freshly painted walls held the scent of chocolate cookies Ikhwani had baked.

"This room is ours," I told Maha.

"It smells funny," she said.

"It smells new."

She smiled.

"Maybe new isn't so bad."

Upstairs, Ibrahim's place mirrored ours—the house split in half, identical and close. For the first time, everyone was under one roof.

There was a bathroom downstairs where we lived. A door that closed. A light that came on.

It was bigger than our kitchen in Ramallah—bigger than anything we had called ours.

The yard stretched wide around the house. But the tall wooden boards held it in—weathered to a dull gray, their backs turned inward like they had something to hide. Along the top, barbed wire sagged in slow, rusted loops. Wind slipped through the gaps and made it hum. I stood at the kitchen window and looked at it for a long time. In Ramallah, the wire was theirs—placed to keep us in. Here, it was ours. And yet my hands remembered what wire meant. My body did not know the difference between a cage and a fence. I was not sure it ever would.

Just beyond, neighbors moved in their own small squares—doors opening, closing—but never long enough to meet a gaze. Sound traveled in pieces: a cough, a chair dragged, a murmur cut short. None of it ever made it over the fence.

I found a bicycle waiting in the backyard—a gift from Ibrahim. Its chrome sparkled. Baba steadied the seat, his hands rough.

"Yalla, go."

"Feel the wind lift you."

I pedaled and the yard blurred and for a few seconds I was not in New Jersey and I was not in Ramallah and I was not anywhere that had a name. I was only moving. That was enough.

Then there was Brandy—a brown German Shepherd with amber eyes. I froze. Her size, her deep bark, her confident stride unsettled me. Ibrahim noticed.

"Go on, Hala."

"She's family."

"I'm scared," I admitted in a whisper.

Brandy lowered her head and nudged her cold nose into my hand. My fear dissolved the way fear does when something warm and certain meets it head-on.

"She likes you," Ibrahim said.

Brandy became my shadow—my courage in fur. If she ever wandered off, I knew exactly what to do: panic.

A few days later, Yamma reached for a small treat left on the counter, took a bite, and frowned.

"These biscuits taste terrible," setting one aside.

Ibrahim laughed.

"That's Brandy's."

She paused.

"No wonder."

That same day, Ibrahim piled us into the car for our first outing. Pathmark stunned us. Boxes stacked to the ceiling, their bright colors making me wonder how one country could hold so many choices—Oreos, Doritos, bright packages that promised tastes I had never had.

"Grab two," Maha laughed, nudging my arm.

She didn't know what they were, and neither did I. Ibrahim bought them anyway. Those Oreos felt like magic—black and white and impossibly sweet, the kind of sweetness that made me feel guilty and joyful at once, as if I had been given something I hadn't earned and wasn't sure I deserved.

Kmart surprised us too—soft fabrics, lamps glowing with warm light, dolls with painted smiles, shelves full of things I didn't know people could own. In Ramallah, we owned little. Here, the world waited neatly on shelves. I walked slowly through the aisles with my hands behind my back, afraid to touch anything, afraid to want too much at once.

A green sign caught my eye—a woman with flowing hair, suspended in green, while steam rose in quiet spirals from the cups in every passerby's hand. The aroma found its way into the car, roasted and sweet, threading through the silence like an invitation.

"What is that place?" Maha asked.

"I don't know," I answered. "It smells... good."

"Starbucks," Ibrahim said.

"Star... shoo, what?" The word tangled on my tongue.

"You'll see these everywhere."

In Ramallah, coffee was a ritual—grounds read, futures traced, time given its proper weight. Here, it was movement. People rushing by with cups bigger than soup bowls, drinking without stopping, without sitting, without anyone turning a cup over to see what came next.

Shadows followed us into the new land.

Maha's illness deepened. Doctors used words I couldn't understand—degenerative heart disease—their voices calm, their faces careful, delivering the verdict the way people deliver things they don't want to carry anymore.

Some mornings, she didn't rise with the house. Her cough carried down the hallway, thin and stubborn. Yamma moved quietly—measuring medicine, smoothing Maha's hair, sitting beside her longer than necessary. I heard her sometimes in the night, the soft sound of her moving between rooms, checking, adjusting, keeping watch.

Their bond tightened in the small hours, stitched together by touch and waiting. I watched from doorways. There are things between a mother and a sick child that no one else can enter. I did not try. I only stayed close enough that Maha would know I was there.

Outside, life kept moving—school bells ringing, buses sighing at the curb.

Somerset Elementary felt older than anything I had known. The long brick corridors echoed with footsteps and the sound of lockers. Classroom doors stood open, nameplates faded from years of small hands brushing past.

There were no school buses. At first, Ikhwani took turns driving me. Over time, I learned the way by repetition—not the town, just the sequence of turns my body remembered. Eventually, I walked.

I sat at a wooden desk scarred by those who had come before me. The teacher's words tumbled past like spilled beads—fast, impossible to catch. I sat very still and listened the way I had listened during curfew: carefully, for anything that might tell me what was coming.

The cafeteria was worse. Long tables stretched across a room that smelled of boiled vegetables and old oil. Children shouted over one another, trading snacks wrapped in plastic. I stared at my tray—a milk carton sweating at the edge, mashed potatoes so pale they looked like paste, chicken nuggets shaped like tiny moons.

Back in Ramallah, Maha and I walked to school together, our hands linked, a simple labaneh sandwich pressed into mine by Yamma's hands—nothing wrapped in plastic, nothing traded across tables. Here, I went alone. Maha remained behind, sick in bed, while I learned a new world without her. That was the loneliness I had not expected—not the strangeness of the place, but doing it without the person who had always done everything with me.

After months, it was decided: Somerset wasn't enough.

I was transferred to East End Elementary School, still in North Plainfield. Ikhwani drove me there at first. I didn't know the way. The streets blurred together, unfamiliar. Later, I learned the road—corner by corner, step by step—until my feet recognized it before I did.

The building felt different from the moment I walked in—louder, more crowded, voices layered in accents I didn't yet understand. Children came from everywhere, carrying pieces of home in their lunchboxes, their language, the way they spoke to their mothers at the door. It wasn't polished. It wasn't quiet. It was alive. For the first time, I did not feel like the only one who was still learning what country they were in.

Teachers knelt to meet my eyes instead of towering above me. Time moved differently here. Some had more than I did. Some had less. I was one of many learning how to belong.

That's when they placed me somewhere else.

They called it special education—the word special lodged inside me like a stone in a shoe.

In my child's mind, special meant riding in the front seat. The biggest slice of cake. The good plate saved for guests.

On my first day, I marched straight up to the principal.

"Is this the class for special girls like me?"

She paused.

"What do you mean by special, Hala?"

"You know," I said, nodding.

"Special special. The good ones."

She closed her eyes. Opened them again.

"Hala," she said gently. "This class is for students who need extra help."

"Oh."

"So... not special girls."

She rubbed her forehead.

"Lord help me."

I nodded, disappointed. I thought I'd been chosen.

My days shifted into hallways echoing with metal doors slamming and teachers calling names I could barely pronounce.

Mrs. Smith, my special education teacher, changed that.

"You're doing so well, Hala."

"Keep practicing."

She said it every day. I began to believe it was true—not because I had proof, but because she said it with her whole face. Some teachers teach subjects. Mrs. Smith taught me that I was worth the trouble of being taught.

I was ten when it happened, in the bathroom at East End School.

I stood frozen, staring down, my body tight, my hands shaking. I thought I was bleeding where I shouldn't be. I went to the principal, then to the nurse's office. By the time I sat on the paper-covered table, the thin sheet crinkling beneath me, I was crying without sound. My ears rang. The nurse knelt in front of me.

Her voice was careful.

"Congratulations," she said.

I looked at her, confused.

"That's your period."

I wiped my face with my sleeve.

"A period?"

"Like the one at the end of a sentence?" I asked.

She paused, trying not to laugh, then explained. Her words moved quickly, slipping past me before I could keep up. I watched her mouth instead, the way it kept going while my stomach twisted and the room tilted. I caught about half of it. I nodded at the rest.

When she finished, she sent me home.

The sidewalks stretched longer than usual. My heart ached as I sobbed, breath catching. I kept my head down, afraid someone would see, afraid something worse was still coming. My body felt like it belonged to someone else—someone older, someone who had been warned, someone who had a mother who sat beside her and explained things in words she could understand.

I was none of those things. I was ten and alone on a sidewalk in New Jersey and I did not know what had happened to me or what would happen next.

Each step felt heavier than the last.

When I got home, Yamma didn't explain it. She didn't sit beside me or tell me what was happening to my body. She tore a strip from a paper towel, folded it, and placed it in my palm.

"Put this in your underwear."

"Go back to school."

That was the end of explaining.

I walked back—confused, afraid, the folded paper towel in my hand like something I'd been trusted to carry without being told what it was for. There are things no one tells you. There are things you learn by surviving them. I added this to the list.

Back at school, everything went on as if nothing had changed.

In chorus class, we learned simple songs that taught us how English sounded before it made sense. The music room had a jumble of instruments along the walls—tambourines stacked in crates, a row of recorders, a piano waiting at the front. Posters of musical notes taped crookedly above the chalkboard.

"Baa Baa Black Sheep" was one of the first. I took it the only way I knew: by repetition, by listening, by letting the words settle into my mouth until they stopped feeling foreign and started feeling like something I owned.

The music room was our routine. We stood in rows. We sang.

Over time, the songs evolved. Christmas carols replaced the simple ones. Teachers discussed an assembly. We practiced more carefully now, the piano louder, the space more focused.

That day arrived. We left the music room and entered the auditorium. Parents filled the space—rows of faces, coats still on, programs folded in laps. The lights felt hotter. The sound carried differently.

I searched the auditorium for familiar faces and found none.

No Yamma. No Baba. No Maha in the seats.

I took my place in the chorus. When the music began, I moved my mouth and pretended I was singing—shaping the words I wasn't sure of yet, hoping no one noticed the silence where my voice should have been. I looked out at the rows of parents and felt the particular loneliness of performing for a room full of people who were not there for you. I thought of Maha on the rooftop, naming clouds. I thought of her saying: keep looking until you see what I see. I kept looking.

I did not find them. But I stayed in the line. I moved my mouth. I let the music carry what I couldn't say.

School brought more than English. It carried responsibility. Parent–teacher conferences came—meetings Yamma could not attend. Ikhwani took her place, shoulders squared in jackets that didn't quite fit. They sat in child-sized chairs while papers slid across the desk between them. They nodded, catching parts, losing others. They didn't go to school—hands leathered from carrying, fixing, building. They had traded classrooms for something else long ago.

Then one day, the words stayed put.

I walked beside Yamma through the school corridor. We sat across from the teacher's desk. The teacher spoke, and this time the words didn't scatter. I caught them. Held them. Turned them into Arabic one by one, and carried them across the desk to Yamma.

I watched Yamma's face change as understanding arrived. The small nod. The way her shoulders settled. The look she gave me after—not gratitude exactly, more like recognition. Like she was seeing something in me she had been waiting for.

I was eleven, and suddenly I had become my mother's voice.

I did not know then what that would ask of me. How many rooms I would translate in the years that followed. How many forms, doctors' offices, phone calls, silences. How the weight of it would sometimes feel like too much, and how I would carry it anyway, because she had carried everything before me.

Outside, the day went on.

Years later, Teta's words stayed with me:

"Remember your roots, Hala."

We had arrived — already cracking. Not breaking. We had been pressed into foreign soil, compacted, cold, and nothing like home. Still, we grew.

Chapter 6

WEEPING VINES

"My guilt has overwhelmed me,
a burden too heavy to bear."
(Psalm 38:4, NIV)

Grief reached me before I understood. It tore out of Yamma—low, guttural—and her forehead struck the wall with a dull crack that shook the frame. Dust drifted down like fine powder. No humming. No clatter. No off-key singing—only the kettle screaming on the stove.

"Why is it quiet today?"

No one answered.

Maha's illness arrived all at once.

Morning light slid across the linoleum kitchen floor. Yamma stirred the tea, the spoon tapping the glass. She bowed her head.

Maha slept through hours that once held candy wrappers and jokes whispered too loudly.

Some nights, I stood barefoot on the carpet, the fibers dull beneath my feet, listening for her breathing. I counted the seconds between each breath the way I had counted Baba's between the soldiers' footsteps. Waiting for the pause that lasted too long. Waiting for the sound that didn't come.

Our days had been loud—secrets smuggled into pockets, songs that missed every note. Now the food sat untouched. Cups refilled, then forgotten.

Yamma's hands shook as she poured.

One night, I heard Baba speak from the doorway.

"She didn't eat today."

Yamma didn't turn.

"She will eat."

As Maha's laughter faded, Yamma's back stayed turned more often. When I entered a room, her hands were always busy—folding, wiping, smoothing. I hovered at the edges the way I had learned to hover during curfew: still enough to be overlooked, close enough to know what was happening. It was a skill I had not meant to learn. It had found me anyway.

Maha showed herself in small ways—a glance held a second too long, a low hum barely audible, a faint smile that didn't quite reach her eyes.

One evening, I moved toward her bed.

The room smelled of medicine and soap. Maha lay turned toward the wall, her hair flattened where it met the pillow, the blanket pulled up too high.

"Maha... can I sit with you?"

She barely lifted her eyes.

"Not now."

The words didn't rise. They dropped—soft, final. The space beside her felt too wide. I looked to Yamma. Her lips kept moving in prayer. I backed away. The hall swallowed me.

It kept going—Yamma's hand on Maha's forehead,

Maha's eyelids fluttering. I carried, cleaned, and fetched while love moved between them, never stopping long enough to reach me.

My name surfaced only when someone needed something. I stayed near the edges, listening to the tap of a spoon against glass, taking up as little space as I could. The door stayed half-closed.

I told myself I understood. Maha was sick. Yamma was afraid. Everyone's hands were full. I told myself this each morning. By evening the telling wore thin, and what was left underneath was something I didn't have a name for yet—something small and hot, pressed down so long it had taken the shape of whatever was holding it.

There was no argument. No single moment I could point to later.

Only the accumulation—days of doorways, of half-closed doors, of love moving past me on its way to somewhere else. I had been invisible for so long that when the feeling finally broke the surface, it came out sideways. It came out wrong.

Heat rose in my throat.

"I wish you were dead."

The room stopped.

Maha turned her head toward me. Something shifted across her face—not shock, not anger. Something quieter and worse. Something that looked like she had been waiting for the world to show her what it really thought of her, and now it had.

She looked at me for a long moment.

"If I die," she said quietly, "don't cry."

I have turned those words over in my hands ten thousand times since. I have held them up to light. I have tried to find a way to make them smaller than they are. I cannot. They are the last real words my sister ever said to me, and they were said in response to the worst thing I have ever said to anyone. That is what I have to live with. Not the grief alone. The order of things.

Yamma didn't speak. She didn't look at me at all. She stepped forward and rested her forehead against Maha's, her lips moving in a prayer meant for God alone.

Fear crashed into regret.

When Yamma finally turned, her eyes were hollowed out.

"Why, Hala?"

"Why would you say that?"

Her voice wasn't angry.

It was wounded.

Those were the last words I said to my sister.

The next morning, Ibrahim and Yamma rushed Maha to the hospital. I didn't go.

School held me in place. A desk. A chair. Chalk dust drifting in sunlight. I imagined Maha small against starched sheets, machines filling the room where our songs had lived—the air sharp and clean, like bleach.

"Why did I say it?"

"Why was I so cruel?"

The questions followed me everywhere. I replayed the moment. Not to understand it—I already understood it. I had been invisible, and invisibility had done what it always does when it goes on long enough: turned inward, turned sharp, turned toward the nearest person.

I knew that. It didn't help.

I learned how to shrink into corners, into pauses between voices, into places where no one had to decide what to do with me. I spoke less and stayed where I was placed. When adults entered a room, their voices passed over me as if I wasn't there. I helped. It was safer than being seen—passing cups, closing doors, standing still when told.

Nights passed without question—where I slept, how long I'd been awake—details that disappeared as easily as I did.

Two months after Maha was admitted, the phone at Abe's carpet store rang, splitting the quiet.

Ibrahim's wife answered.

Her face changed before she screamed.

I ran toward her.

"Maha's gone!"

"Gone where?"

"She died."

The words landed in pieces. I heard them one at a time, like something dropped from a height, each one striking the floor separately before the whole shape of it became clear. Even then I stood still for a moment, waiting for the next part. There was no next part.

Tears came hard and fast, spilling before I could stop them. We closed the shop and rushed home.

I didn't know Yamma hadn't heard yet. The words left my mouth anyway.

"It's okay, Yamma."

"We're all going to die."

She turned to me.

"What are you saying?"

The truth hit her. I watched it move across her face the way weather moves across open ground—nothing to stop it, nowhere to go. Yamma's face fell inward.

She pounded her cheeks, letting out a scream. She slammed her forehead against the wall until the plaster cracked.

I had seen her do this once before—the day grief first entered our house in Ramallah. Then, I had not understood the fullness of what she was feeling. Now I did. And I knew something else: the last words I had given Maha were ones I could never take back. Yamma's grief was pure. Mine had a shard of guilt running through the center of it, and I had put it there myself.

I stood where I was.

The house began to fill—women arriving with scarves half-pinned, shoes kicked off and left crooked by the door. Someone gave Yamma a glass of water, her hand shaking. Another dragged an empty chair closer. Voices rose and fell in fragments—prayers, names, instructions. Everything moved faster than I could follow.

By the time we reached the funeral home, everything had already been arranged.

A wooden coffin rested at the front. People touched it

as they passed. Women cried openly, their grief loud and uncontained. Men stayed rigid, jaws tight, holding everything in. The room smelled of flowers and something else—sweet and wrong.

Guests gathered near Maha. Hands reached out, careful, as if she were only sleeping and might wake if startled. She was there—too still, too quiet. Her hands were folded. Her skin looked waxy.

Sitting across from the casket, I thought I saw her smile.

That's when I went to her.

My legs felt hollow. I leaned close to her face.

"Wake up, Maha."

"Please... wake up."

She didn't.

I had said the wrong last words to her and now I could not say any better ones. There is no correcting the record with the dead. They leave with whatever you gave them last. I have had to find a way to live inside that. I have not always managed it.

Outside, the procession formed. The coffin was lifted and carried over the shoulders of men who had known her—men whose faces were controlled and wet at the same time. A horse-drawn carriage waited ahead, its wheels still, its presence quiet and heavy.

I sat beside Baba, where I felt closest.

At the gravesite, the coffin was lowered into the ground. Yamma broke beside me. Her voice tore through the air. She reached forward, her hands grasping at nothing as others held her back. The sound of her crying didn't stop. It filled everything—the trees, the cold ground, the space between people who didn't know what to do with their hands.

I stood there, my chest tight, something breaking open inside me that had no sound attached to it. Yamma's grief poured out. Mine stayed in. I did not know then that grief you cannot release does not leave. It waits.

After the burial, the days blurred together. Meals appeared, then vanished. People filled the house, then slowly stopped coming. The rooms stayed heavy even when empty. I waited for someone to say we were finished. Finished mourning. Finished crying. No one did.

Grief didn't leave.

It became furniture.

Traces of her still moved through the house—the dip in her pillow, the way her scarf shifted when the door opened, as if someone had passed through.

One Sunday, the radio crackled to life. A song came on "Pictures of You" by The Cure. I didn't know the band. I didn't know the words. The first notes were enough. Tears came before I could stop them. I didn't try. Some songs find the exact shape of what you cannot say and hold it for you. That one did.

When that song finds me, I break.

Maha's last words stayed with me.

"If I die, don't cry."

They didn't comfort me. They sat there—heavy, unmovable—like a stone in a pocket. I was crying anyway. I had been crying since the carpet store. I have been, in one way or another, crying since.

Nights filled with weeping—prayers breaking apart in Yamma's throat, footsteps dragging across the worn rugs. Some mornings, she couldn't rise from bed.

I slipped out of mine and went to her, reaching for her hand.

"Yamma?"

She turned her face toward me, eyes swollen, hollowed by loss.

"Ana asfa, Yamma. I'm sorry."

"Ma kunt aqsid. I didn't mean it."

She turned away. Her hands shook. Her breath faltered.

Yamma moved through the days without seeing me. I understood it. The person she was looking for was not in the room. She was looking past everything that remained toward the one thing that didn't. I had done that too, standing in doorways, looking past what was there for what I wanted. I could not be angry at her for the same hunger.

Alone, I stood at the bed where Maha used to lie. Dust gathered on the mantel. Nights stretched long and hollow.

Some evenings, Yamma sat on the floor rocking. Sobs broke out of her in pieces. Then chanting—fractured, urgent.

"God, help me..."

"God, help me..."

At night, I lay awake listening for it, afraid its return meant something worse was happening to her. I had already lost Maha. The thought of losing Yamma—not to death but to grief, to the place grief takes people when it goes on too long—was a fear I could not name out loud. I lay still and counted her prayers instead of her breaths, the same way I had once counted Maha's.

In the kitchen, voices gathered. I heard Ikhwani say her sisters' names. I heard Ramallah. They said she needed to be with Tamam, with Jamila, with Teta. Suitcases appeared from closets and corners. No one explained anything to me.

Yamma was gone longer than I could measure.

Days passed without her voice calling my name. I slept without her checking the door. I ate at the table without her. At night, the house stretched wider than it used to, corners dark and watchful. I listened for footsteps that never came.

I learned the weight of the keys in my hand, how to lock the door before bed, and how to sit still in silence.

Maha was dead.

Yamma was in Ramallah.

The house held the same silence.

Fear came quietly.

It made itself at home.

There was no one left to keep the house.

There was only me.

I was twelve when they pulled me from school.

My books stayed on the desk. The bell rang without me. Recess secrets ended mid-sentence. The chalkboard was left half-erased. The smell of sharpened pencils and clean paper belonged to someone else.

What I knew closed its door.

Duty opened another.

At first, I thought school was only paused—something I would return to once things settled. I kept my books stacked neatly. My pencils stayed sharpened. I told myself this was temporary the way you tell yourself anything is temporary when you cannot bear for it to be permanent.

Days passed. Then weeks. No one spoke of going back.

One morning, it became clear. The world beyond the walls moved. And I was no longer part of it.

Some afternoons, children's voices drifted in—shouts rising and falling, sharp with play.

"Why can't I be out there?"

"Just once."

"I wish I could be a kid too."

I stood at the stove, stirring pots too heavy for my arms. Steam fogged my skin. The mop dragged behind me, leaving dull streaks across the floor. The walls took over. With Yamma gone, I checked the cooktop twice before bed. I folded laundry before anyone asked. By morning, the house was clean and quiet—proof I was useful. Proof I deserved to stay.

Days folded into one another—wake, work, silence, sleep. My body moved before I thought. Hunger came and went without asking.

Ikhwani came home, boots striking the floor. Onions hissed in the pan, sharp and familiar.

Sometimes, light broke through. Bike rides beneath thick trees. Swims in the backyard pool, water flashing blue in the sun. Garage-sale finds—old books, bent toys, things that smelled like paper and rust. A stolen grape burst tart on my tongue. Small mercies. They mattered. I held them the way you hold warmth in your palms in winter—knowing it will go, holding it anyway.

The rules tightened without warning. Curfew snapped shut—no longer from the street.

"What did I do to deserve this?"

"Maybe this was my punishment for wishing my sister dead."

The thought arrived without warning and stayed without invitation. I turned it over the way you turn a wound—not to examine it exactly, more to check whether it was still there. It always was.

At night, when the house finally went still, I lay awake staring at the ceiling. The words surfaced. I pulled inward, arms wrapped around myself. Some guilt doesn't announce itself. It seeps. It finds the cracks left by grief and moves in quietly, and by the time you notice it has settled, it has already been there long enough to feel like it belongs.

I stood at the sink, washing dishes while Ikhwani worked. Green Palmolive coated my hands, bubbles clinging to my wrists, the clean scent rising with the steam.

Then a voice said my name.

"Hala."

Warm. Close. Like breath against my neck.

"Hala."

More urgent.

"Hala."

I turned.

Maha stood framed in the doorway between the living room and dining room—solid, unmoving, unmistakable. She looked straight at me. Not through me. At me. The way she always had.

My breath snagged.

Her shape. Her eyes—exactly as I remembered. Not fading. Not drifting. Not imagined. Present the way only real things are present—occupying space, displacing air, demanding to be seen.

I thought: she came back.

Then: she is dead.

Then: she is here.

The three thoughts arrived in the time it takes to blink, and none of them could exist alongside the others, and all of them were true.

Fear hit.

The plate slipped from my hands. It shattered on the linoleum, shards skittering like startled insects. The sound broke the stillness of the whole house.

I didn't think.

I ran.

Glass burst behind me as I slammed through the door. I tore across the yard and hauled myself up the eight-foot fence, wire biting into my palms. I dropped hard onto the grass on the other side, my knees burning, my vision tilting and swimming. My body wouldn't stop shaking. It had made a decision before my mind had finished catching up, and it was not going to apologize for it.

My breath jerked as footsteps crunched nearby. A

neighbor rushed over, drawn by the noise. She found me crumpled on her lawn—grass-stained, gasping, my hands scraped and shaking. She knelt beside me and pulled me gently upright, guiding me in as the screen door creaked closed behind us.

"Hala, sweetheart, what happened?"

"Did someone hurt you?"

"No... I'm not okay."

"She's in there."

"Who's in there?"

"Maha."

"I saw her. I heard her voice."

"It's okay."

"Just breathe."

When I tried to explain, the story broke apart.

"My sister came back."

"She called my name."

The neighbor's eyes widened. She clasped her hands together and nodded once.

"I believe you, Hala."

I do not know if she did. But she said it. And she said it without hesitation, without the pause that means a person is deciding whether to be kind or honest. She just said it. It was the first time since Maha died that I felt someone had received something from me without taking it apart first. I stopped shaking.

She stayed with me until my shaking slowed.

When Ikhwani came home from work, she told them she'd found me crying and shaking on her lawn.

They looked at me.

Then they looked at each other.

"It's an excuse."

"To avoid the house."

The words cut through me. They didn't ask what I'd seen, or why I was shaking, or whether I was afraid. They turned away, finished with it. I stood in the kitchen and understood something I had been circling for months: being disbelieved is its own kind of erasure. It does not leave a mark. It simply removes one.

I stayed with what I knew—pulled from school, buried in work. I waited for Yamma, counting the days. I needed her to put her hands on my face and tell me it was real—or tell me I was safe. Either one. I would have taken either one.

I replayed it. Her voice. The doorway. The way she looked at me.

No one asked me to tell it.

So, I didn't.

I kept it folded in me, afraid that if I spoke it out loud, it would be taken from me too.

I waited for Yamma the way I had waited for Maha—measuring time by absence.

Two months later, Yamma returned.

Her suitcase wheels whispered across the floor. The sound reached me before she did.

I ran to her without thinking. After standing in doorways—watching her give every breath to Maha—my body moved before fear could stop it. I needed her arms. I needed her voice. I needed Yamma.

The story spilled out of me—the voice, the doorway, Maha calling my name, the panic. I didn't slow it down. I didn't soften it. I gave it to her the way I'd been holding it: whole, and shaking, and too long kept.

Yamma didn't interrupt. She pulled me into her, her cheek resting against the top of my head. I felt her inhale. One long breath, taken all the way down.

When she spoke, her eyes were already full.

"She called me too."

"On the plane."

"Through the engines."

"Yamma... Yamma."

Her voice shook. She walked the aisle, scanning row after row for a child who wasn't there. The engines drowned out everything else. When she realized it was Maha, her knees buckled. A flight attendant had to guide her back to her seat.

We sat together with that.

Maha had found us both—separately, across distance, through the noise of engines and the silence of empty rooms. She had called the name of the person she needed, and we had each heard it, and we had each run toward it, and we had each had to be guided back.

I thought about the last thing she said to me. Don't cry. And here we were, the two of us, crying. I think she knew we would. I think that was why she said it. Not as a command. As a permission. A small, quiet release from the obligation to hold it in.

I let Yamma's arms be the place where it landed. Outside, nothing softened.

They called it safety.
I called it confinement.
The answer was always no.
I lay awake, staring at the ceiling, leaning on Maha.
Morning came.
Nothing changed.
Except me.

Chapter 7

Stirring Shoots

"You hem me in behind and before;
you lay your hand upon me."
(Psalm 139:5, NIV)

No windows lined the classroom. Fluorescent lights hummed above us, relentless, desks bolted into rows.

The air smelled of chalk and dust. I sat still, hands flat on the desk. I kept my eyes lowered until the bell rang. New Jersey buses hissed along wet pavement. Lockers slammed and kids scattered.

"Take out your notebooks," the teacher said, her voice flat, chalk tapping the board.

"She's crying again," a boy muttered.

"Leave her alone," another answered.

I didn't look up.

My teacher smiled.

"You're doing better, Hala. I'm proud of you."

Her words caught me off guard. I didn't know what to do with them. Praise, in my experience, was a door that could close as quickly as it opened. I held it carefully, the way you hold something borrowed.

After school, I walked home, counting cracks in the

sidewalk. Bikes flashed past me, spokes clicking, laughter trailing behind them. A boy shouted a name that wasn't mine.

"God, please help me."

I prayed.

Ikhwani burst in, then out—shoes thudding, voices loud, pockets full of time. The screen door slapped shut behind them. I stayed in the kitchen, homework spread neatly in front of me, the chair legs cold against my calves. From the table, I could see the clock above the sink—the second hand moved. I did not.

Ikhwani returned flushed and hungry, talking over one another as they dropped into chairs. No one asked where they'd been. No one asked why. No one told them no.

"Be back later," they called.

"Don't wait up."

When I asked Yamma, the answer came quickly.

"Girls don't go out."

"School is enough."

"You have everything you need right here."

The lights went out, and Yamma moved through the house like she was made of prayer. Some nights I heard her chanting through the thin walls—quiet, relentless.

"Yamma?"

"Sleep, Hala," her voice cracked on the last word.

The house carried Maha's absence. As grief deepened, Yamma retreated. Ikhwani filled the space she left—stricter than ever, convinced discipline held the family together.

"Where are you going?" I asked, sitting on the porch

steps.

"For a ride."

He didn't ask if I wanted to go.

During recess, girls clustered outside the bathroom door, breathless with plans.

"Chorus rehearsal tonight."

"Roller-skating at the rink."

"My mom said yes to the sleepover."

Their words bounced off the tile, easy as coins tossed in the air.

"I have to go home."

My afternoon stretched tight. I stood at the window as bikes blurred past, my fingers at the glass. Kids gathered at the bridge across the street. Someone slipped and laughed. Someone else yelled,

"Wait for me!"

Some weekends, voices floated through the screen door.

"Hala, can you come out?"

"We're riding to the park—come with us!"

Before I could answer, Yamma's voice cut through from the kitchen.

"La', mish mumkin, it's not possible," she called.

Their bikes clattered away, wheels ticking. I stood at the door long after the sound was gone, my hand still on the frame, the space where they had been already closing over.

From the kitchen, my name snapped the air.

"I'm just watching."

"Watching turns into wanting."

She wasn't wrong. But she had the remedy backwards. The watching didn't create the wanting. The wanting was already there. It had always been there. The watching was just what happened when a girl had nothing else to do with it.

As a teenager, the home rules hardened. School ended, and I went straight home. No dances. No football games. No rides with friends. I passed girls in the hallway smelling of hairspray and excitement, their dresses folded carefully in gym lockers.

"Are you coming on Friday?"

"I can't."

My footsteps sounded loud, each step a reminder of where I was allowed to stand. I moved from room to room with nothing to do but wait. While my classmates whispered about movie nights and sleepovers, I set the kettle on and folded towels, carefully aligning each edge.

We moved often—from one roach-infested house to another. Different streets. Different addresses. The same rules. I memorized them the way other kids memorized phone numbers—where to stand, where to stay, how not to get attached.

"Why can't I be like them?"

I asked again, standing in the doorway, shoes still on.

"Why can't I go out with my friends—just this once?"

Yamma didn't raise her voice. She never had to.

"It's not for you."

"You're not like your brothers."

She turned toward me then, her face calm, certain.

"They're men."

"You're a girl."

"And it's a scary world out there."

Her words settled into the room, final. There was no space left for another question. I looked down at my hands, small and empty, heat rising sharp enough to sting. I knew better than to argue. Yamma loved me. I never doubted that. But love, in that house, came with a blueprint. And the blueprint had no room in it for a girl who wanted to ride a bicycle to the park on a Saturday afternoon.

Punishment came fast.

Sometimes loud. Other times quiet.

A wooden spoon cracking against skin.

A belt snapped through the air before landing.

A door slammed so hard the walls jumped.

Other times, silence answered. Days without a word. Meals passed without looking at me. My name withheld like oxygen.

Bruises bloomed and faded beneath my clothes, yellowing at the edges. I wore long sleeves in warm weather—not for modesty, but to hide what I couldn't show.

What I learned, in those years, was how to go somewhere else while staying exactly where I was. Not dreaming—something more controlled than that. A withdrawal so practiced it became reflex. The sound of a belt was still in the air when I was already gone, already in the place inside myself where nothing could reach me. I came back when it was over. I straightened my sleeves. I went on.

That is a skill no child should have to learn. I learned it anyway. And I carried it long after the house stopped requiring it, the way you carry a posture your body adopted in a cramped space even after the space has opened.

The fear stayed longer, and I learned how to disappear.

Talking to boys was taboo. Wanting space was also discouraged. Even time with other girls was monitored. Too much closeness implied influence. Losing control. I stayed within the lines. My hands were always busy.

I sat beside Yamma at the table, folding grape leaves tight and neat, one after another—scoop, roll, tuck.

Kibbeh took shape in my palms, smoothed carefully so nothing cracked. I carried bags, made phone calls, and spoke for her in places she couldn't.

The kitchen stayed warm. Onions hissed as they hit olive oil. Cinnamon and cumin bloomed in the air. Pots murmured on the stove, lids trembling slightly, as if they were trying to speak.

I scrubbed counters, ran errands, and translated the world. English belonged to me. The world outside belonged to me—but only on Yamma's behalf. I carried her through every door I was not allowed to walk through on my own. That is a particular kind of freedom: boundless for someone else, borrowed for yourself.

In the evenings, Baba sat at the table with me. A dictionary lay open between us, pages worn gentle with time. He pointed to a word, sounded it out slowly, then looked up at me for approval.

He was my earliest compass.

Arabic curling toward home. Years later, our hands switched places on the page. By the mist of tea, I traced English beneath his weathered hand, letter by letter.

"You're getting better at this, Baba," I told him.

He smiled.

Sometimes we turned it into a game. Cards and dominoes spread across the table. His brow furrowed in concentration. When he lost, he shook his head, amused with himself.

"You tricked me."

"I didn't," I said, grinning. "You just didn't like losing."

He let out a soft laugh, like the whole world had room for mistakes.

The walls loosened. The air softened. I wasn't careful. I wasn't quiet. I was just there—his daughter, teaching him words, sharing the table, breathing freely. In those hours, I was not a girl managing the distance between herself and punishment. I was not a girl watching the clock. I was just a person at a table with someone who loved her without conditions attached.

Those moments didn't last—nothing ever did.

I held onto them anyway.

There was a science fair at school.

I told Baba I needed a project. He paused, eyes drifting toward the shed, then snapped his fingers.

"A bell."

"A bell?" I asked.

He nodded and moved ahead already. We cleared a corner of the porch and spread out the parts on an old towel—springs, screws, metal smooth from years of wear. He showed me how the springs and screws fit together and how pressure made a sound. When a piece didn't catch, we paused, leaned in, and tried again. Grease smeared my hands.

The bell rang sharply as we tightened the final screw.

It won Best in Show.

Baba stood beside me as they announced the winner, his smile quiet and unmistakable—victory belonged to both of us. I had not expected to win. I had expected to try, which was what he had taught me, which was, I understood then, the same thing.

To celebrate, we slipped into a theater for Rocky, sharing popcorn in faded black seats, the music swelling as I cheered for more than just the fighter.

"Take more, Hala," he whispered, nudging the bucket toward me.

"It's so good," I said, wiping salt from my fingers.

He leaned in, eyes soft.

"See? Life doesn't always have to be rocky."

I smiled into the dark.

After he got his driver's license, he took me for a drive. The windows were down. People on the sidewalk lifted their hands, waving wildly.

Baba laughed.

"Look, Hala—everyone is so friendly!"

I looked ahead.

"Baba..."

"You're going the wrong way."

He slammed on the brakes, eyes wide. The horns blared behind us, and our laughter burst out louder than the noise as he swung the car around. I laughed with him, the kind that steals your breath and surprises you with its own arrival. The kind that has no audience. The kind that is entirely, completely yours.

As a child, I wanted to be a nurse. Then Baba cut his finger, and I screamed loud enough for the neighbors to hear. He wiped his hand, shook his head, and said,

"Hala, nurses don't scream louder than the patient."

I laughed so hard I forgot he was bleeding.

Those moments ended the way they always did—quietly. Baba stayed near me when he could—at the table, on the porch, in the passenger seat. Beside me, never in front of what ruled.

Yamma and Ibrahim brought control. Baba brought joy. It never lingered. But it was real, and it was mine, and no rule in that house could reach back and undo it.

I was afraid of disappointing Yamma or Ibrahim. Just the daily fear of getting something wrong—a missed chore, a tone that slipped, a pause before answering.

"Did you finish the dishes?"

"Yes."

"Don't forget the bathroom."

I followed the rules like instructions I didn't remember agreeing to. The house grew quiet in the afternoons.

The television became my hiding place.

I turned it on low and sat close, knees tucked in, the glow filling the room. Luke and Laura's fiery romance on General Hospital stirred me.

"Don't do it," I whispered once, leaning forward.

They did it anyway.

Later, the channel changed. Erica Kane stood tall on All My Children—unapologetic, saying what she wanted. I watched her closely, memorizing the way she held herself, as if the world made room for her because she decided it would. She did not ask. She did not wait. She did not fold herself smaller so others could be comfortable. She stood in the full width of herself and let the room adjust.

I had never seen a woman do that in real life. I filed it somewhere deep, in the place where you keep the things you intend to grow into.

I imagined speaking. Standing like that. Turning away when something didn't serve me. Deciding.

When footsteps approached, I muted the sound. When a shadow crossed the doorway, I sat straighter.

"What are you watching?"

"Nothing."

The screen went dark. The itch stayed.

"One day, I'll have my own life," I told the glass.

Even then—especially then—I believed freedom waited beyond the walls of that house. I didn't know what it looked like. I didn't know when it would come. I knew it existed, the way morning follows night. Erica Kane had shown me the shape of it. Baba had given me the laugh of it. Maha had held the hand of it. I was collecting evidence. I was building a case.

One day, my uncle, who worked at a diner, looked at me and said,

"Apply for the open position."

He took me with him, with Yamma's permission.

Scotch Wood Diner gleamed in the New Jersey sun, chrome siding flashing light back at the street.

At fourteen, I stood outside the doors, my reflection caught in the glass—a small girl framed in red. A neon sign hummed:

Breakfast All Day. Homemade Pie.

Fried air drifted when the door opened.

"You can turn back."

My hand closed around the handle. Sweat gathered in my palm. My heartbeat pounded, urging me forward.

The world opened.

Cozy booths. Bright lights. A menu stretching across American, Greek, and Italian favorites. Old jukebox selectors sat on every table—little chrome boxes waiting for a quarter.

A waitress in a crisp apron and a paper cap angled just right leaned over a booth and said,

"Coffee, tea, or me?"

The customer laughed. She winked like she'd said it a thousand times. She had the ease of a woman who had decided, long ago, that the room was hers.

Right then, I knew—this was where I belonged.

The air smelled of bacon, eggs, and brewed coffee. Vinyl booths creaked beneath shifting bodies. Plates clattered against a constant hum. Mike and Art—the owners—looked me over.

"You're hired," Mike said.

Order tickets flashed. The bell above the kitchen window rang sharply. I set tables, lined silverware, poured drinks, and shadowed servers, learning the rhythm of it all.

Mike had an easy charm that softened the shifts, even when Yamma later claimed half my pay. The job gave me a way out.

I couldn't drive, so Mike pulled up outside the house in the afternoons. I waited on the steps, watching the car idle.

"Ready?"

He leaned across the seat to open the door.

"Always."

The rides were quiet. The road stretched ahead. The house fell away behind us. That short distance felt like motion instead of stillness. It felt like a preview of something I didn't have a name for yet but recognized the way you recognize a word you've heard before you know what it means.

Two years passed. After my shift one evening, Mike waved me over to the register.

"You've been steady," he said. "You don't miss shifts. You learn fast."

He slid a paper across the counter.

"Host. Cashier. And a raise."

I stared at it.

"Thank you," I said.

My voice didn't shake.

Behind the counter, I stood straighter. I greeted

customers. Counted change. Balanced the drawer at the end of each shift. People began asking for me by name.

"She'll help you."

"She knows what she's doing."

I rode home with my pay folded tight in my hand, my fingers pressing against it. Outside the house, I was someone who knew what she was doing. Inside, I was still trying to prove I deserved to take up space. The distance between those two people was the distance I spent those years trying to close.

Sometimes, I asked Yamma if I could walk to the thrift store down the street. A candy bar slipped easily into my hand. An ice cream cone melted faster than I could eat it. Once, I bought a shirt with the original tags still on it. I held it up in my room later, smoothing the fabric between my fingers before hiding it in the drawer. The next day, I wore it proudly. Each purchase was a quiet declaration—just enough to be mine.

In the evenings, I crocheted, sitting on the edge of my bed or at the small table by the lamp, yarn pooled at my feet.

The needles clicked softly—steady, patient—the one sound I could control. Loop. Pull. Tighten. The yarn slid through my fingers, warm and yielding, taking shape without argument.

No one rushed me there. The house faded. Stitch by stitch, it grew.

I grew.

I was choosing colors when I could not choose where to go. I was choosing patterns when I could not choose who to see. I was deciding when to stop and when to keep going—and those were small decisions, yes, but they were mine, entirely mine, and nothing in that house could unravel them once they were set.

When the blanket was finished, I spread it across the bed and smoothed it flat with both hands. The rows lined up. The edges held. I stood back and looked at it.

A woman passing by noticed my crocheted blankets, her eyes fixed on the one draped over my knees.

"Are those for sale?" she asked.

I nodded, surprised.

"How much?"

"Fifty dollars," I said.

"I'll take it," she said, smiling as she handed me the bills.

It was my first sale. I slipped the bills into my piggy bank. I stood there for a moment after she left, the money in my hand, understanding something new: I had made something from nothing, and someone had wanted it, and they had paid me for it, and no one had been in the room when it happened. It had been entirely between me and the woman and the blanket and the fifty dollars. It had been mine.

I made another blanket. Then another. Each one left my hands and went somewhere else—into another house, onto another bed. The making was the point. The choosing was the point.

Still, I listened: a footstep in the hallway made my shoulders tighten; a voice calling my name pulled me back too quickly. The yarn waited where I left it, needles stuck mid-row.

"Don't forget," Yamma said. "There are expectations."

Chores filled the day. I picked the needles back up anyway. Each stitch set. Each row held. What once felt protective tightened, and the small freedoms I had gathered slipped one by one.

That afternoon looked ordinary.

I came home with my bag still on my shoulder, the weight of school still in it — a worksheet half-finished, a book I had been meaning to read, a pencil worn down to its last inch.

The kitchen smelled of coffee. A cup sat on the counter, untouched. The clock above the sink read half past three. Nothing was cooking. The silence of the stove.

Baba was already at the table. He did not look up.

Arabic music was off. No dishes clattered. The house held the particular stillness of a room that has been waiting.

"Sit."

Yamma's voice came from the table, leaving no room for questions.

I set my bag down slowly. I thought she might ask about school. I arranged what I would say — the worksheet, the teacher's comment, something ordinary to fill the silence with. I was practiced at filling silences. I knew how to make a room feel less heavy by handing it something small.

She didn't ask about school.

She stared.

HALAINA

"I've found a husband for you."

Chapter 8

TORN STEMS

"When you pass through the waters, I will be with you;
when you pass through the rivers,
they will not sweep over you."
(Isaiah 43:2, NIV)

Yamma stood there, calm. The refrigerator hummed.

A faucet dripped once, then stopped. The linoleum felt cold under my shoes.

"A husband?"

"Yamma, I'm sixteen, in high school, and working. Are you serious?"

I turned toward Baba.

"Baba, please—talk to her. I think she's gone crazy."

"You'll learn to love him," Yamma said.

"Like you loved Baba?"

"You'll understand one day."

"Understand what? There's nothing to understand. You're giving me away."

"A mother protects her daughter, even from herself."

"Like you protected Maha."

Her eyes went flat, as if she were seeing something behind me—not me.

"Let her finish school," Baba said. "She's still a child."

"You think too softly," she snapped. "The world doesn't wait for girls."

The word girls landed like a slap. Not daughter. Not me—girls.

"Do I even matter?"

The room didn't answer.

I felt left behind—school, independence, choice, moving on without me. Images flickered through my mind: college brochures, graduation caps, a bedroom I chose for myself, my name on my own door. Then they burned and blew away.

The kitchen felt wrong. The family photos blurred—smiles, holidays, people who didn't know what was coming. My hands shook against my thighs.

I turned to Ibrahim.

"Why are you doing this to me? I don't even know which is worse—that Nicholas is family or that he's my second cousin. How am I supposed to be with someone I don't love? I'm begging you. Please don't do this."

Ibrahim had always been my refuge. Now he was part of the sentence—silent when I needed him to be my brother again. I looked at his face, waiting for the version of him that had said Always when she asked if I was coming. That Ibrahim did not show up. The one standing in the kitchen said nothing, and his silence was its own kind of answer.

My voice broke apart as I spoke, shrinking until the words might miss me.

No one moved.

The old rules wrapped around my throat like they'd crossed the ocean with us. I wouldn't finish like my classmates. Their lives moved forward while mine sealed shut. Yamma had been pulled from girlhood early, her future decided before she knew to ask for more. Nelly's marriage had been arranged at fifteen. Now it was my turn—different country, same sentence.

I pressed my palm to my sternum as the room warped around me. The edges of the table swam in my vision.

That night, in the dark, I thought if I took enough pills, everything could stop—not life, just the noise. The noise of a future already being decided. The noise of a girl who had collected evidence and built her case and now watched it mean nothing. I swallowed them in the bathroom with the light off, because I did not want to see my own face. I did not want to be seen at all. I just wanted the noise to stop, even for one night, even for one hour.

When I woke, machines tracked my heartbeat. Their beeps marked time while decisions continued without me. The emergency room smelled of blood and something stale. Bright lights pinned my eyes open, curtains never fully closed, a nurse's shoes scuffing past. A paper bracelet sat loose on my wrist, sliding just enough to remind me I was there.

No one from my family said: we heard you. No one said: we will change something. The engagement marched forward as if my body hadn't just begged for mercy. I lay in that hospital bed and understood something I had been refusing to understand: the asking was over. I had asked every way I knew how. This was what came after asking.

Nicholas insisted on taking me to a hotel, calling it a "special surprise." I said yes, even as my stomach twisted before we reached the door. The hallway carpet swallowed our footsteps. The keycard clicked. The door opened into cold air.

Nicholas pinned me down and raped me.

I stayed frozen. My skin burned. The carpet scraped my knees as I went rigid. I counted the carpet's pattern and named objects in the room—lamp, dresser, curtain, TV. Anything to stay somewhere else. That is what the mind does when the body cannot leave: it goes ahead without it. It finds a corner of the room that is only geometry—shapes and colors and names—and it stays there until it is over. I have never fully come back from that corner. Part of me is still in it, counting.

Afterward, I stared at the ceiling, hoping it might open and let me out. Nicholas leaned close, his breath hot and sour.

"If you tell anyone, I'll lie," he hissed. "I'll say you begged for it. Your family will believe me."

His voice lingered longer than his touch. I stayed there, eyes open.

My family kept the doors locked—no boys, no laughter too loud. Purity was the only proof I mattered. No one taught me what to do once the danger was already inside, and everyone called it safety. Just like when I got my first period, Yamma handed me a folded paper towel and walked away—no explanation, no comfort. I stood in the bathroom shivering, waiting for someone to tell me I was okay. I was still waiting.

Silence felt safer.

I confided in a neighbor. My voice trembled as I told her what Nicholas had done. She wanted me to report him, but I couldn't. In my world, speaking out meant danger; my family would have hurt me before believing me. She didn't press me. She grabbed her keys.

"Come on. Let's go."

At the free clinic, the paper gown crinkled under me as the nurse spoke softly, her words heavier than I could bear.

"You're pregnant."

She handed me the test. Two lines.

I kept the results from both my family and Nicholas. The timing before the wedding let me hide it. The wedding drew near, and I carried terror beneath my skin—a second heartbeat. I didn't know which was worse: what he had already taken or what would still come. Now I was expected to perform a lie on top of a violation—to prove my purity with blood on a sheet. My body, which had already been taken from me once, was about to be inspected for evidence of its own theft.

My marriage took place in Bethesda, Maryland, in a cold Lutheran church that smelled like old hymnals and floor polish. The organ groaned through my ribs as more than two hundred fifty guests filled the pews, watching me walk down the aisle in borrowed gloves, my palms slick with sweat. The vows stuck in my throat like chains cinched around my neck.

The air in the church held a sterile hush—faces I didn't know, smiles that didn't reach the eyes, applause that sounded like a play. I stood in white, my breathing louder than the vows. During the ceremony, I drifted through my own wedding, nodding when hands squeezed mine and smiling for pictures. My body was there. I wasn't.

When the ceremony ended, Nicholas leaned toward my family and assured them,

"Don't worry. I'll take good care of her."

I watched my family receive those words. I watched them believe them. I understood then that some promises are made to the wrong people—offered to those with the power to accept them, not to those who would have to live inside them.

On our honeymoon in Orlando, the park buzzed around us—kids laughing, fireworks crackling, caramel and popcorn drifting sweet and warm. That evening, when I hesitated to undress, his smile faded.

"Don't test me," he snapped.

The slap came, and heat burst across my cheek. The room tilted, and somewhere down the hall, ice clinked in a cup.

His jaw clenched as he grabbed the keys. Minutes later, anger simmering off him, he drove us down a dark stretch of highway—no lights, no signs, just the road unspooling into black. Without warning, he jerked the wheel toward the shoulder, gravel spitting under the tires.

"Get out."

"It's the middle of nowhere," I murmured.

"Out."

I stepped onto the gravel, the cold night air hitting

my skin sharp and immediate. He sped off, his taillights shrinking until they disappeared. Silence pressed in. My heart hammered. The night smelled like exhaust and damp grass. Cars hissed past somewhere beyond the dark, never close enough to see. The shoulder felt too narrow, the road stretching beside me.

There were no voices, no movement—just my heartbeat, loud and hard, and the sound of my own breathing, which I kept listening to the way I had once listened for Maha's—to prove that something was still continuing, that I was still here, that the night had not yet closed all the way over.

A sound tore out of me before I could stop it, raw and sharp, breaking open the night.

"Ya hayawan, you animal."

Hours later, he came back. His face was smooth and serene, as if nothing had happened.

"Get in."

I got in. My cheek ached with every heartbeat. Maha running her fingers through my hair, Baba laughing as he waved at honking cars, Yamma quietly giving me a folded paper towel on the day I had my first period—all of it felt distant. Not gone. Distant. Like a country I had been deported from and was no longer allowed to enter.

"This is the promise you made to my family?" I whispered, more to the windshield than to him.

Back at the hotel, he pointed to the floor.

"You sleep there."

The carpet was rough under my arms, and cold air

from the vent blew in steady bursts, scraping my skin. The bed's white sheets glowed untouched. They would look for blood. I had to give them something.

Nicholas moved me into his family's musty basement—a low-ceilinged cave beneath his overbearing mother and disabled brother. The air smelled of damp concrete and rot. Boxes sagged in the corners, cardboard soft with moisture. A single bulb buzzed overhead, casting a faint yellow circle that barely reached the walls. I stood with my suitcase, staring at the mattress against the wall. The basement felt like a place for storage and forgotten things. I understood, without being told, that I was both.

A week after settling in, I wasn't a new bride. I was an inmate. I moved through the basement doing housework while his mother hovered close enough to breathe down my neck, her eyes tracking my hands.

"You're washing the dishes wrong."

I was expected to live in darkness.

Upstairs lived Lina, my sister-in-law, my only breath of fresh air. She moved through life boldly, laughter spilling out of her as if nothing could dim it. One evening in her small kitchen, she leaned in and said,

"Don't let her talk to you like that."

Her kitchen smelled of garlic and lemon, real food simmering on the stove—food that tasted like life. In Lina's company, pieces of myself returned in small, fragile bits. I had not realized how far I had gone until I felt myself, briefly, come back.

Later, she set a plate in front of me as if she were feeding a person, not a prisoner.

"You're stronger than you think," Lina said.

Her words didn't fix anything. But they steadied me for one more day. Sometimes one more day is everything.

A month after the wedding, Baba called, his voice full of excitement about his upcoming trip to Jerusalem. I finally gathered the courage to tell him,

"Baba... I'm having a baby."

His joy poured through the line, warm and proud.

"Take care of her," he told Nicholas.

"Take care of my baby girl."

I held the phone after he hung up and listened to the silence it left. His voice had been the same as always—full of the laugh he gave away freely, full of the love that had no conditions attached. I had not told him what the marriage was. I had not wanted to take that particular thing from him. I let him believe I was all right. It was the last gift I could give him.

A week later, the call knocked me to my knees.

Baba was gone. Fifty-three years old. Dead.

My family arranged to go to the funeral in Jerusalem. Baba had always wanted to be buried there.

"I have to go," I told Nicholas. "I need to say goodbye. I need to be with my family."

"You're not going anywhere," he said flatly, his face unchanged.

"You're staying."

I stood in front of him and understood something about cruelty—that it does not always announce itself loudly. Sometimes it arrives in a flat voice and an unchanged face, as if the thing it is refusing you is not important enough to raise a hand over. That was the one that stayed. Not the slaps. The flatness. The face that looked at my father's death and found it small.

My throat tightened until I couldn't swallow. I stared at photos—Jerusalem's red earth piled over Baba's body, my uncles lifting him, their faces twisted with sorrow. He had taken my last chance to honor Baba. The man who had driven the wrong way down a one-way street and laughed until the tears came. The man who had stood beside me at the science fair with his quiet, unmistakable smile. The man who had been beside me, never in front of what ruled.

I held the pictures tight and cried until the fabric swallowed my breath. I have not stopped mourning that absence. Not the death—I would have mourned that anywhere. The not-going. The red earth I never stood beside. The goodbye I never got to say out loud.

While I was still grieving, Nicholas opened Chicken Basket in Rockville using my savings and our wedding funds. He never asked. I worked beside him—laying tile, handing him tools, doing whatever he needed to open it.

"Come on," he said one morning, tossing me an apron. "I need you there."

My back throbbed, and my feet pressed painfully against my shoes. The sticky floor tugged at each step while customers smiled as if nothing were breaking. Fryer oil clung to my hair, skin, and clothes, following me home.

It was one of those days when the radio played "The Living Years" by Mike + The Mechanics. A song about a son who never said what needed to be said before his father died. I froze, my hand still wrapped around a wet glass. The words landed in the place where Baba still lived—the place that had not yet accepted that he was gone, that was still waiting for the phone to ring with his voice on the other end. I did not move for a long time. The glass grew warm in my hand. Around me, the diner went on—orders called, plates stacked, the bell above the window ringing—and I stood inside it, completely alone, saying to no one everything I had not said while he was still alive to hear it.

He worked me long hours while I was pregnant, my feet swollen and aching. A customer asked as I leaned too long on the counter, my hand pressed to my lower back,

"Sweetheart, are you okay?"

"I'm fine," I said, forcing a smile.

I was six months pregnant with Adam when Nicholas beat me until I collapsed, my hands over my belly as I prayed my baby would live.

Adam arrived at eight months, tiny and jaundiced, glowing under blue lights in the NICU. I delivered alone.

The nurses noticed the bruises.

"What happened?" one asked.

"I... I fell."

"You fell?"

"Yes. I fell."

The room went quiet. She looked at me the way people look when they know the answer and are asking anyway, hoping this time will be different. I looked back at her the way people look when they know they are not going to say the true thing, not because they don't want to, but because the true thing will not keep their children safe. She understood. She did not push. I watched Adam through the glass, my body bruised and stitched, my heart aching.

When they finally placed him in my arms, I wept into his hair. He was warm and small and entirely himself, already, before he had any reason to be. I held him and thought: you did not choose any of this. Neither did I. But here we are. And I am not going to let this be where we stay.

Nicholas showed up to pick us up as if it were another errand.

Routines tightened around me.

Laundry came first. Water was reused until it turned gray. The soap thinned out. Clothes were lifted heavy and sour, slapped against the sides of the tub, wrung out by hand. Nothing was ever clean—only wet again.

His mother pointed at the basin, cloudy with soap scum.

“Bathe him,” she said.

I looked at it, the smell hitting the back of my throat. Adam slept in my arms, warm and light, his skin still faintly blue from the hospital.

“I’m not bathing him in that.”

She didn’t look away. Nicholas moved before anyone could speak. The first punch knocked the wind out of me, then another. I hit the tile hard, cold shock rushing through my spine. My ribs throbbed when I tried to move.

Adam cried—sharp and panicked—and I twisted so his head stayed clear, my arms locked around him. I stayed on the floor until his crying softened and his breathing found rhythm again. Then I stayed a little longer, just to be sure. The floor was cold. I did not care about the floor.

Three months after Adam's birth, I was pregnant again, not out of love but from assault. My body hadn't healed, and the violence continued.

Lina and I were pregnant at the same time. She carried to term; her third girl came home the next day. Ramone didn't. He arrived early at six months, when Adam was nine months old—a two-pound, hummingbird child. Machines breathed for him, his tiny chest rising and falling beneath a forest of tubes and wires.

A nurse leaned over the incubator to adjust the tubes. Another glanced at the chart and looked back at me.

"He can't come home until he reaches five pounds."

I nodded.

My days split between the hospital and the basement where Adam waited. I didn't trust leaving him in my mother-in-law's care, but I had no choice. In the NICU, monitors beeped and plastic chairs pressed cold against my legs. I stood at the incubator, my finger resting against the warm plastic.

"Just keep breathing, habibi, my darling."

Ounce by ounce, Ramone fought. I counted each rise and fall. He was teaching me something, in that incubator, though I did not have the words for it yet: that the will to continue does not require understanding why.

It only requires the next breath. And the next. And the one after that.

At night, beside Adam, I lay awake listening to his soft whistle in the dark, afraid that sleep might take him. His face in the morning—creased from the pillow, lashes matted with sleep—was proof worth guarding.

When Ramone finally came home, my body wanted to fold. I fed them both, sometimes one on each side, their mouths searching, their cries overlapping. I learned how to stand back up because they needed me to stand.

I was nineteen, with two children and pregnant with the third, my body changing without permission. Days stacked on top of each other—bruises fading, new bruises blooming. Sleep broke under fear, but it wasn't louder than their breathing. I moved through the house quietly, counting what might buy an hour of peace. As long as my boys were near me, I kept moving.

Sometimes Lina and I went out with the strollers, side by side, the wheels rattling over cracked sidewalks under gray skies.

"Slow down," Lina said. "If you walk any faster, the strollers are going to file a complaint."

"Fear makes a good pace-setter."

"Good," she said. "Then we're not slowing down."

We ended up at a diner—cracked vinyl booths, fogged windows, voices humming around us like we weren't there. I stared at the tabletop, my hands empty, tracing the dull Formica where other people had dragged their forks.

"I can't keep living like this," I said. "In that house, downstairs. No windows. With his mother watching everything I do."

"I understand," Lina said. "You can't let her get to you."

She didn't offer a plan. She stayed, letting the clatter of plates and the scrape of chairs fill the silence until my breathing slowed. That was enough. That was, some days, everything.

That night, I watched Adam and Ramone sleep. Adam's breath was soft and steady. Ramone twitched in his dreams, his fists opening and closing as if he were already fighting something. If I stayed, this would be their normal. This would be their childhood. They would grow up thinking a basement was what a home looked like. They would grow up thinking a man's raised fist was what a father looked like.

"I have to find a way to leave."

The chance came on an ordinary day when Nicholas and his family were out of the house. Hesitation was already gone.

I gathered diapers, clothes, and bags half-zipped, grabbed shoes without a match, and carried the kids one by one to the car, their eyes wide and quiet in a way that frightened me. Children know. They always know. They were quiet because they understood that this was the kind of moment that required quiet, even before they had words for what the moment was.

My hands shook so badly I dropped the car keys—once, then again. I crouched and found them by feel, blinking hard as my vision swam. I had no money—just the three hundred dollars Lina kept folded beneath the linens in her drawer. I stayed a second too long. Taking it felt wrong, but leaving without it was impossible. I took the money. I have never stopped being grateful for that money. I have never stopped being grateful for Lina.

Nicholas had deliberately kept me from getting a Maryland license, reminding me I couldn't go anywhere without him. My hands trembled as I turned the ignition, but I pulled out anyway.

At a stoplight, I caught their faces in the rearview mirror. Adam gnawed on his sleeve. Ramone stared out the window, trusting me without knowing why. That trust was the most terrifying thing I had ever been given. It was also the thing that kept my foot on the gas.

I pressed the gas.

The airport was loud, bright, and unforgiving. I counted bills twice. It wasn't enough. I couldn't hold both boys on my lap, and panic lodged in my throat. A woman looked at me, then at the boys, and nodded once.

"I'll hold him," she said.

Adam sat on my lap. Ramone sat on hers. I bought one-way tickets to New Jersey.

Safe, I told myself.

When we landed, the weight hit all at once. I dialed Lina's number.

"I'm sorry. I took the money. I didn't know what else to do."

There was a pause. Then her voice came, calm.

"It's okay. You did what you had to."

My body gave out as pain tore through me without warning. I curled forward, my hands locked over my belly. Samuel came early.

The hospital hummed—monitors ticking, voices low, carts rattling past. I stared at him, small and fragile, breathing. I had run as far as I could run, and here was the place I had landed, and here was this child who had arrived in the middle of the running, before we had even found a door to go through. I did not know how to keep him safe. I had not managed to keep myself safe. But I looked at him, and he was breathing, and I was breathing, and for that moment it was enough to just be two people breathing in the same room.

Then the room phone rang. My family had called Nicholas and told him where I was. My stomach turned cold. Even here, even now, they had handed me back.

I lay there, listening to the hospital, my child beside me.

Nicholas picked us up and dragged us through broken houses—peeling wallpaper, sagging ceilings, cracked tubs. I stopped unpacking anything except diapers and whatever scraps of hope I could salvage. I woke tired. Morning light felt like an accusation. He beat me, and I carried it on my skin.

Then came a Saturday night I will never forget.

Nicholas stumbled in late, drunk and high on cocaine. The living room light made his face look slick and unfamiliar, like it belonged to a stranger. Adam's toy truck sat upside down near the couch. Ramone's blanket was wadded in a corner. The house smelled like cold grease and old heat.

"Where's my dinner?" he roared.

"I'm making it," I said, panic tightening in my chest.

The pot clanged. A fork slipped from my fingers and hit the counter with a sharp, helpless sound. He didn't wait. He grabbed the yellow telephone cord and looped it around my neck.

My hands clawed at it, nails scraping plastic. I could not get air. I could not get air. I could not get air. Then it loosened enough for one breath, and one breath was enough to move, and I moved.

I broke free and bolted for the door, running into the night. The cold hit my face like a slap. A porch light snapped on. A neighbor's screen door creaked.

"Young lady... are you okay?" she called. "Come inside, it's cold out there."

"I can't," I tried to say, but the words wouldn't line up.

Her house was warm, smelling like fresh-baked cookies. She said her family was at a church event and that she wanted something nice waiting. I shook so hard my teeth clicked. She pressed a glass of water into my hands and sat close enough that her shoulder touched mine.

"Breathe," she said.

I told her what Nicholas had done. I had left my three boys behind. She prayed out loud and wrapped her arms around me until my body finally gave up the holding. There are people you meet for ten minutes who change the shape of a night. She was one of them. I did not even know her name.

When she walked me home, the street looked the

same. The house lay in pieces—keepsakes on the floor, photographs facedown, glass everywhere, crunching under my shoes.

The boys were crying—one clinging, one stiff with shock, one too still for his age. I gathered them close.

"Mama! Mama!"

Their voices hit me harder than any fist. Not because of the fear in them—though the fear was there. Because of the reaching. Because even in the middle of all of that, they were still reaching for me. They still believed I was the thing that would make it better. That belief was the only thing in that house that had not been broken.

I held them tight and understood something clearly: he could break objects. He could not have my boys.

After that, the house became a trap. New locks, no spare key, no easy exit. Nicholas moved through it like a man who owned the air. Weeks passed in a quiet that wasn't peace, only a pause.

Then it started again.

One night, he knocked a plate to the floor and leaned in close.

"Clean it up," he spat. "With your mouth."

Then he grabbed Adam too roughly, too fast, and I saw the cigarette press into his skin.

"No," I screamed.

Something split open in me that never closed again. Not rage—something older and quieter than rage. A decision. The kind that doesn't announce itself, doesn't ask permission, doesn't wait for a better moment. It simply arrives and takes over.

That night, my children slept beside me, their small

bodies pressed close. Adam whimpered in his sleep. I laid my palm against his back and rocked him, waiting for the pain to let go. It didn't.

"We are leaving."

The next morning, I waited until Nicholas went to work. I called Ibrahim. His wife answered.

"What do you want?" she said.

"I just need help."

"Two hundred dollars."

"Anything."

Silence stretched.

"We can't," she said, and hung up.

No one was coming.

I stood in the kitchen for a moment after the line went dead. I had asked the last person I could think to ask. Ibrahim, who had placed his hand on my shoulder and said Always. Ibrahim, who had jingled his keys and looked down at me and said Yalla, Hala, let's ride through town. He was not coming. The version of him I had believed in—the one who chose me—was not going to walk through the door. I put the phone down. I stopped waiting.

I grabbed the birth certificates, Social Security cards—anything with our names on it. The paper felt sacred in my hands, the way the permit had felt in Baba's hands on the street in Ramallah—the proof that we existed, that we had the right to move through the world. I took a chair and swung it through the window. Glass shattered. Blood ran down my knuckles, but I didn't stop.

I lifted the children through the frame one by one and climbed out after them. The outside air hit us hard.

We moved fast without looking back.

A school bus stopped at the corner. I flagged it down. The driver looked at me and then at my children.

"Get on," he said.

He drove us to the police station. They called social services. A "safe house," they said.

It wasn't.

The hallway smelled of mildew and cigarettes. Women sat with empty eyes. Doors slammed. Someone shoved me into a wall.

"Watch your back."

I pulled my children close and made myself a shield.

At night, windows rattled. Men's voices drifted outside. Packages hit the glass. Smoke filled the air. I slept with my eyes open and fed my children in the dark.

I told the staff what was happening. They nodded and went back to their clipboards.

One evening, I sat on the bathroom floor and pressed my wrist against the sink until blood ran. I wasn't trying to die. I was trying to make something on the outside match what was happening on the inside, because I had run out of words, and I had run out of asks, and there was no one in that building looking at me long enough to see that I was disappearing. It was the wrong way to ask for help. It was the only way I had left.

They bandaged me and sent me back.

After four months, they ended our stay and handed me three bus tokens.

Cold circles in my palm.

No plan.

No one.

Chapter 9

MERCY'S TENDRILS

"Because of the Lord's great love, we are not consumed,
for his compassions never fail. They are new every morning."
(Lamentations 3:22–23, NIV)

My three hungry boys sat beside me at a bus stop with nothing but cold air and nowhere to go. The tokens dampened in my hand. The metal bench pressed cold into my spine as traffic roared past without slowing.

The wind burned through my coat, the sky the color of old dishwater. Adam leaned against my side, Ramone pressed his head into my ribs, and Samuel sagged heavy in my arms. Their weight was the only warm thing.

We had been kicked out of the safe house that morning. No warning. I kept rolling the tokens with my thumb, counting and recounting, as if the number might change.

Nicholas could find me—the thought landed sharply, the way it always did, arriving before I could prepare for it.

I looked at the street, then at my boys.

Adam was gnawing on his sleeve. Ramone's eyes were half-closed, the way they got when he was past hungry and had stopped asking. Samuel breathed against my collarbone, warm and trusting, his fist curled around the lapel of my coat.

They did not know where we were. They did not know there was nowhere to go. They trusted me the way they always had—completely, without evidence, without asking what I had done to deserve it.

That trust was the thing that had kept me moving. Sitting on that bench, I felt it shifting.

If he was going to find us anyway, I could decide how it ended.

I began watching the buses differently—not as transportation, but as timing. How fast they moved. How much space there was between the curb and the lane. I watched and I calculated and I held my boys and I did both of those things at the same time, and that is the thing about that morning I have never been able to fully explain: how a person can love something completely and still be standing at the edge. Those two things were both true. I was both of them at once.

If no help came, I would step off.

Somewhere between that decision and the next breath, a woman sat beside me.

One moment, the bench was empty.

Then she was there.

I did not hear her arrive. I did not see her sit down. She was simply present, the way warmth is present when a door opens into a heated room—not announced, just suddenly undeniable. She looked at me the way almost no one had looked at me in years: as if I was still here. As if being still here mattered.

"What's wrong?" she asked gently.

Everything spilled out. Nicholas. The violence. The shelter. My family's silence. The fear that never loosened its grip. The tokens in my hand. The boys asleep against me. The buses I had been watching. I did not plan to say all of it. I had not said all of it to anyone. It came out the way things come out when you have been holding them alone for too long and someone finally looks at you directly—all at once, in no particular order, with no dignity left to protect.

She listened without interruption. She did not flinch. She did not look away.

When I finished, she leaned closer.

"Stop whatever you were doing," she said.

"There's a program. You need to go to this address."

She pulled a slip of paper from her coat and pressed it into my hand. Her fingers were warm. I noticed that—the warmth of them, on a morning that cold.

"Only the first fifty are accepted," she continued. "You need to get there."

I looked down at the address, the paper trembling between my fingers.

I looked beside me.

She was gone.

Not walked away. Not standing at the corner. Gone—the bench empty beside me as if no one had ever sat there. I looked up and down the street. I looked behind me. There was no one. The boys had not stirred. No one nearby seemed to have noticed her arrive or leave.

I sat with that for a moment.

I have sat with it for the rest of my life.

I am not going to explain it. I am only going to say what is true: she was there, and then she wasn't, and she had left something warm in my hand, and the calculation I had been making at the edge of the curb had stopped.

For the first time that morning, something loosened. Not hope—curiosity. Just enough to move.

The bus pulled up. I dropped the tokens into the slot one by one and climbed the steps. The doors folded shut behind me. I did not look back.

The address led to a worn office building tucked between tired brick and cracked sidewalks.

Nothing about it looked like a rescue. The paint peeled, the air smelled stale. I considered turning around. Instead, I walked in.

The room was quiet. An oscillating fan clicked in the corner. Then a voice called my name.

A woman stepped out from behind a desk and motioned for me to sit. She opened a folder and slid it toward me.

"You're here about the new program," she said calmly.

I stared at her.

She repeated what the woman at the bench had told me—the same program, the same limit. Word for word. As if they had spoken. As if someone had called ahead.

A chill moved through me. I had told no one where I was going. I had not known where I was going until twenty minutes ago. I had a slip of paper and a bus token and three boys, and somehow this woman behind this desk in this peeling building knew why I had come.

She continued as if nothing was unusual.

"If you qualify, we'll cover a thousand dollars in housing."

She slid the form toward me.

"Sign here."

The pen felt heavier than it should have. I thought of everything that had brought me to this desk—every door that had closed, every person who had said we can't, every morning I had woken up inside a life I had not chosen. I thought of the boys on the bench. I signed.

The ink dried. She closed the folder.

"You're in," she said.

"In what?"

"You were the fiftieth applicant."

That morning, I was calculating how to end our lives.

By afternoon, I was holding a housing certificate.

I do not have a clean explanation for what happened between those two facts. I only know that something reached into that morning and changed the direction of it. Call it what you need to call it. I know what I call it.

That same afternoon, I searched the newspaper and found a modest two-bedroom in Germantown.

It was seven hundred. I could make that work. I called the landlord and asked if I could see it. He agreed. When we met, I explained that the money would come directly from the program—that it was guaranteed, that rent would never be late. I told him I had three boys and nowhere else to go. I prayed while I waited for his answer. Not elaborate prayer—just the inside of my chest turned upward, asking.

He studied me for a long moment, then nodded.

Yes.

His name was Joe Reiber. I repeated it to myself the way I had once repeated the names of streets I was learning—carefully, so it would stay.

The apartment wasn't large. Plain walls. Bare floors. It was enough. More than enough. It was the first place in years that was mine to lock from the inside.

We stepped into that empty apartment with only our clothes on our backs, a certificate, and a promise. No beds. No furniture. No dishes. Just space.

The boys' voices echoed against the walls, bouncing back at us. They ran from room to room as if the air itself had changed. Adam pressed his palm flat against the wall as if testing whether it was real. Ramone spun in the middle of the empty living room, arms out, laughing at nothing. Samuel sat down on the bare floor and looked up at me with an expression I had not seen on his face before.

Peaceful. He looked peaceful.

I stood in the doorway and let myself feel the size of the room. The absence of his footsteps. The absence of his voice. The locks on the door that only I had the key to. I had not understood, until that moment, how much of my body had been listening—constantly, involuntarily—for the sound of danger. Standing in that empty apartment, the listening stopped. The quiet was not the quiet of holding still and waiting. It was just quiet.

A neighbor noticed us that first evening. I knocked on her door and asked if she had anything I could use to feed my boys. She didn't hesitate. She handed me what she could and later offered to watch them when I found work. I did not know her name yet. I knew only that she had opened the door, and that mattered more than I could say.

Food stamps were approved. Churches opened their doors. Sale by sale, we gathered what we needed—one chair, a small table, and dishes that didn't match.

Blankets that smelled faintly of other homes. A couch with sagging cushions. A kitchen table with one uneven leg. Lamps that hummed faintly when switched on.

Piece by piece, it began to look like something lived in. It wasn't elegant, but it was ours. Every mismatched dish, every sagging cushion, every humming lamp had been chosen—by me, for us, without asking permission from anyone.

The first night, we slept on the floor. The boys curled into me, their breathing quiet. The apartment was silent—no shouting, no footsteps, no doors slamming in the dark. The locks held. The boys slept through the night.

I lay awake and listened to them sleep. Not the way I had listened for years—braced, counting breaths, waiting for what came next. Just listening. Just grateful. I watched the ceiling lighten as morning came, and I did not feel afraid of it.

I stopped scanning the window and started scanning the newspaper.

After we moved into the apartment, I met Nancy through the program—a headhunter with sharp eyes and a softer voice than I expected.

I walked into her office and shook her hand, my grip limp.

"No, sweet girl. That won't do."

She took my hand, firmed my grip, and squared my shoulders, showing me how to meet someone's eyes without shrinking. I had spent years making myself smaller—in doorways, at tables, in rooms where the wrong posture cost something. Nancy was teaching me to take up space again. To let my body say: I am here, and I am not asking your permission.

She took me to a clothing bank and pulled suits from crowded racks. The fabric felt structured. Different from everything I had worn in that basement, in those broken houses, in the years of other people's definitions of what I was for.

I studied myself in the mirror and barely recognized the woman looking back.

Not polished. Not confident.

Beginning.

That word arrived quietly and settled. I had ended so many times—the school desk cleared, the window broken, the bench at the curb. I had not let myself think of any of it as beginning. Nancy, with her firm handshake and her crowded clothing rack, was insisting that it was.

I chose to believe her.

With her help, I found two part-time jobs—early mornings waitressing at Bob's Big Boy and afternoons answering phones at Colquitt Caruthers, a real estate firm. One taught endurance; the other taught voice. Together they taught me that I could hold more than one thing at once and not drop either. I had always known how to work. Now I was learning that the work could be mine.

No one handed me credentials.

I watched. I showed up early. I left late. I learned anyway.

A woman from the newspaper came weekly to collect the ads I prepared. I asked about her job, and she spoke of freedom—of setting her own schedule, of moving independently.

Freedom. I rolled the word in my mouth the way I used to roll bus tokens in my palm. Testing its weight. Deciding whether I believed it was something I was allowed to have.

I decided I did.

A few weeks later, I applied to the Fairfax Journal and got the position. I learned to sell ads by listening carefully and stepping forward even when my voice felt small. The voice grew. Not all at once—gradually, the way anything grows when it is finally given room. I stopped asking permission. Not loudly. Not in any way anyone else would have noticed. I just stopped waiting for someone to tell me I was allowed to proceed, and

proceeded.
She arrived with her hair pulled back. The skin on her hands was rough, and her knuckles were thickened as if they had done hard work for years. Her nails were clipped short, clean and unpolished.

"I'm Mary."

Her name felt familiar. Like I had heard it before. Like it belonged to the same category of things as the woman at the bench—things that arrived exactly when they were needed and asked nothing in return.

Mary moved into our rhythm without force—cooking, folding, holding my boys with the calm of another teta, someone who understood that children need to be held as much as they need to be fed. She did not ask about the bruises that had faded. She did not ask about Nicholas. She simply showed up and stayed, and her staying was its own kind of answer.

She handed me her car keys.

"Use it."

Borrowed miles meant fewer buses, fewer late arrivals, fewer explanations. The days widened. I drove to work in a car that was not mine, wearing a suit from a clothing bank, selling ads for a newspaper, and I was the freest I had ever been. That is not a small thing. That is everything.

Weeks later, I went back to the office to thank them.

The windows were boarded. The door locked. The place looked like it had been abandoned for years—not months, not weeks. Years. The kind of abandonment that accumulates slowly, that weathers and fades and does not happen overnight.

I stood on the sidewalk in front of it for a long time.

I thought about the oscillating fan clicking in the corner. The woman who had known my name before I said it. The form I had signed. The fiftieth applicant.

I thought about the woman at the bench—the warmth of her fingers, the slip of paper, the empty space where she had been.

I did not understand it. I did not try to. There are things that happen in a life that do not fit inside an explanation, and forcing them into one diminishes them. What I knew was this: on the morning I had stopped believing anything could change, something changed. Something arrived. Something pressed a piece of paper into my hand and said: not yet.

I walked away from the boarded windows and did not look back.

None of it was sudden. It was earned.

One door, then the next.

Chapter 10

Hardening Roots

"We are troubled on every side, yet not distressed;
we are perplexed, but not in despair;
persecuted, but not forsaken;
cast down, but not destroyed."
(2 Corinthians 4:8–9, NIV)

THE INVASION

For a while, it felt like we had outrun Nicholas. The apartment held. The locks stayed quiet. The boys learned where the light switches were. Adam claimed the corner of the couch. Ramone lined toy cars along the windowsill. Samuel slept with his hand wrapped in my shirt.

I stopped watching the street every time a car slowed outside.

Mercy showed up in small movements—a ride when I needed one, a meal waiting on the stove, a door unlocked without questions. I wasn't healed. I was alive. For a time, that felt like enough. For a time, it was.

Peace came cautiously.

Mornings came with routine. Aprons, orders, steaming coffee cups. I went to work that morning, balancing plates, refilling glasses. The hum of chatter and the clatter of silverware almost felt safe.

Once, I had stood behind a counter as a girl.

Now I stood there as a mother of three.

My manager appeared at the counter, his expression breaking that calm.

"You have a call," he said.

His tone chilled me. I wiped my hands on my apron and lifted the receiver.

"Nicholas found us."

"He's here," Mary was screaming.

My heart slammed.

I dropped the phone and ran. I didn't say a word to anyone. Headlights streaked past as I drove, my hands tight on the wheel. I heard the boys before I even parked—their cries cutting through the air.

The front door stood open. The house sounded wrong, split open by sobbing and shattering glass.

"Mary!" I shouted.

No answer.

Nicholas turned on me. He grabbed my hair and yanked me back, his grip iron and unforgiving. The ceiling spun. My scalp burned. My boys were crying, the sound sharp and panicked. I couldn't reach them. A plate shattered against him.

"Stop hurting Mommy!" Adam screamed.

Someone called the police. Flashlights cut through the wreckage, white beams bouncing off walls and glass. By the time officers moved in, he was gone—slipping into the morning.

The officer looked at me and didn't soften his voice.

"Get a gun," he said.

I stared at him.

The next day, my hands still shaking, I walked into a pawnshop. The man behind the counter laid several on a cloth without asking why I was there. He could see why I was there. I bought a small .38 Special revolver. Heavy in my hand. Cold against my palm.

That night, it lay on my nightstand.

I stared at it and prayed I would never use it. I understood, for the first time, what it meant to be willing to. Not eager—willing. There is a difference. I had spent years being someone things were done to. The gun did not make me powerful. It made me present. It said: I am here, and there is a line, and this is where the line is. I prayed I would never have to say it out loud.

I stared at the ceiling until the room went gray with morning.

I waited, listening for her footsteps, watching the street.

Mary never came back.

I secured a state grant for childcare—a small reprieve that loosened the constant knot in me. With the grant approved and income coming in, I went to the dealership and signed papers with hands that no longer shook. The insurance went through—no violations, no accidents. When I drove off the lot, the wheel firm beneath my palms, I felt something return to me—movement. The particular freedom of being able to leave.

I couldn't keep them from Nicholas—by law, he still had visitation rights. That didn't change. Each time I handed them over, my body went rigid. All I could do was pray and wait until they came back through the door, count their limbs, check their faces, hold them until my breathing slowed.

Later, while the boys were visiting Nicholas for the weekend, I finally used the time. I needed space. To think. To make calls. To look for legal help without him knowing. The house felt too quiet without them, the silence pressing in from every side. That kind of quiet has its own weight when you are used to listening for small bodies breathing in the dark.

On Sunday afternoon, I called to arrange pickup. He told me to meet him at the restaurant we once owned. His voice was calm, almost casual. The hair on my arms lifted.

Chicken Basket was packed. Heat and noise rolled out from the kitchen. Grease hung in the air. The moment I stepped inside, my stomach dropped.

Nicholas lunged.

His arm locked around my neck. He dragged me toward the fryer. Oil bubbled and hissed beside us, the heat blasting my face. My feet scraped uselessly against the tile as he forced my head down, closer, closer.

"Please, Nicholas, don't," I said, my voice breaking.

The receiver came out of nowhere. It slammed across my face. My jaw exploded.

A flash of white pain. Blood flooded my mouth, hot and metallic, pouring down my neck as I collapsed to the floor.

When I came to, the sound was far away, underwater. My jaw screamed. My vision split. I forced myself upright and drove home on instinct alone, blood soaking my clothes.

I drove back to the condo and went straight to the bedroom. The revolver caught the light on the nightstand. My hands shook as I loaded it. When I arrived at his address, he was gone. His car was missing.

I was not going to die here.

I got in my car and headed toward the hospital, my jaw swelling, blood running down my neck. Halfway there, the road blurred. I slammed into an electric pole—metal folding, glass exploding.

Hospital lights. Jaw wired shut. My body bandaged.

I drifted in and out of consciousness, the ceiling sliding away and back again. The blow still pulsed through my face. Metal cinched my jaw shut. Each breath scraped. I tried to swallow and couldn't.

My wrist wouldn't move. Cold metal bit into my skin.

Handcuffed to the bed.

Nicholas had pressed charges.

I lay there, beaten, wired shut—and I was the one restrained.

I stared at the ceiling. The cuff on my wrist. I had driven myself to the hospital through a jaw that no longer worked and a windshield that no longer held. I had survived what had just happened. And I was the one in handcuffs. I did not have words for what that was. I still don't. I only know that something inside me—something that had bent and bent without breaking through all the years of that marriage—looked at that cuff and decided, with absolute clarity, that it was the last thing that would ever hold me in a place I had not chosen.

Each breath hurt.

I kept breathing.

The door opened.

Two officers stepped in. No questions. No explanation. One of them unlocked the cuff. The metal slipped free.

They turned and walked out.

I lay there for a moment in the after of it—the wrist suddenly light, the absence of the metal more present than the metal had been. Some things you don't understand until they are removed. I flexed my fingers. I looked at the ceiling. Then I looked at my hand, free and still.

I was going to have to do something with it.

THE WIRING

Amid the fog of medication, the hospital staff arranged for lawyers to assist me.

Because of my extended stay, my boys were temporarily placed with their father. I felt the absence like a physical thing. Their voices, their footsteps, their small bodies pressed against mine—gone. I counted the days in the particular way you count days when each one feels like a debt you are owed.

A counselor introduced me to a lawyer willing to take my case pro bono—sharp-eyed, calm-voiced, a beacon in the wreckage. She filed for divorce immediately and fought to bring my sons back to me. I trusted her the way I had learned to trust the people who showed up without being summoned. There are people who arrive exactly when they are needed. I have stopped being surprised by them. I have only started being grateful faster.

Four weeks later, I was discharged. My body was still bruised. My jaw still wired shut. I couldn't open my mouth. I couldn't speak—but I was no longer the one being held in place.

Everything went through a straw: thin broth, watered-down juice, pain pills crushed and bitter, sticking to my tongue. Drool escaped if I wasn't careful. Each step felt deliberate. I kept my teeth clenched, my hands steady.

The silence was different now. Not the silence of being shut out. The silence of a jaw held closed by metal while the mind runs free. I had things to say. I was learning, again, that having things to say and being able to say them are not the same. I had learned that before—in other rooms, under other conditions. This time the wire was literal. This time it had a removal date.

I held onto that.

When I got home from the hospital, an eviction notice hung crooked on the door.

The paper flapped when I touched it. A red stamp ordered me to vacate within thirty days.

My knees gave way. I caught myself on the doorframe, holding onto the only thing that hadn't been taken yet. My hands trembled as I read it. The condo association had labeled his violence a "liability." Because of him, the boys and I were evicted. I stood there with the notice in my hand and thought: he is not even here and he is still doing this. The damage did not require his presence to continue.

Still healing, my jaw locked for months to come, I packed without speaking. I folded clothes. Wrapped dishes. Gathered toys from corners and boxes.

I dropped to 95 pounds.

Then came court.

I stood before the judge with my jaw still wired shut, metal pulling at my face when I swallowed. He looked at me once—really looked—then turned his attention to Nicholas.

The courtroom stayed silent.

"I never want to see you in my courtroom again."

He paused.

"You're lucky I'm not locking you up today."

The gavel came down. The divorce was finalized. I regained custody of my boys—five, four, and three.

They had waited for me that day, legs swinging from a hard bench, shoes scuffing the floor, eyes fixed on the doors. When I finally walked out, divorce papers folded tight in my hand, they rushed to me, wrapping themselves around my legs, careful and fierce all at once.

Adam stood back slightly and looked at my face. Not the wires—my face. The way a child looks when they are trying to understand something too large for them, and they are going to try anyway.

"Did Baba do this to you?"

Ramone stepped closer, his voice quieter.

"I'm sorry, Mama. You're hurting?"

Samuel reached for my chin with sticky fingers, confused.

"Baba is a bad man?"

I nodded. I tried to smile without moving my mouth.

They stared at the wires, their faces tight with worry.

"We love you, Mama."

"We're going to protect you."

I could not speak. My jaw was wired shut. So I pulled them in, all three, and held them in the courthouse hallway while people moved around us. I let their words go into me the way warmth goes into cold hands—slowly, then all at once.

They were five, four, and three years old and they were offering to protect me. I had been trying to protect them since before they were born.

We stood there holding each other up, and I understood that this was what we were—not a mother and her children, exactly. Something more mutual than that. Something forged in the years behind us, carrying us through everything still ahead.

When I held them afterward, their weight in my arms felt right.

He still had visitation rights.

I found a modest house with a fenced yard and signed the papers with my mouth still wired shut.

The first time the boys ran outside, I watched from the sliding glass door. Their feet pounded the grass, laughter cutting through the air. A fenced yard. Their own grass. I had chosen it. I had signed for it with a jaw that couldn't open and hands that were finally, for the first time in years, not shaking.

I couldn't speak to the boys. People on the phone could not understand me.

I couldn't take it.

I used pliers.

I will not dress that up. I sat on the bathroom floor and wrapped the pliers around the wire and pulled. The pain went white and total, filling every corner of my skull. I did not stop.

My boys were outside and I could not call to them. I had been silent for long enough, and the silence was no longer something being done to me—it was something I was choosing to end.

The wires had been put there by a surgeon to save my jaw. I understood that. I pulled them anyway. By then, silence felt like the one thing I could not survive one more day of.

I ended up back in the hospital. My jaw wired shut again.

Another month passed.

After four months, the wires were finally taken out. My jaw refused to cooperate—muscles stiff and unwilling, opening only a little at a time, week after week of pain to stretch it wider. Eating hurt. Smiling felt strange.

Healing wasn't a moment.

It was a slow process, measured in millimeters and months.

But the wire was out. The silence was mine to break or keep, on my own terms, in my own time.

I opened my mouth.

I spoke.

THE RETURNING

Around that time, I placed an ad in the Fairfax Journal for a roommate and found Derek.

He was kind—especially to my boys. He moved in and made himself at home in the way that good people do: quietly, without demanding that you rearrange yourself around them.

Nicholas kept showing up.

Each exchange tightened my body, my shoulders locking as I handed my sons over and counted the minutes until they were back in my arms. Their hands wrapped around my fingers when they returned. Their weight leaned into me at night. We needed each other to stay upright.

At night, their voices rose soft and familiar,

Five little monkeys jumping on the bed,

one fell off and bumped his head...

Mama called the doctor...

and the doctor said...

No more monkeys jumping on the bed.

Then quieter—four... three... two... one... none.

I lay there listening, my body still, counting them the way I counted everything—breaths, minutes, the time they were gone, the time they were safe again. None was the best number. None meant all accounted for. None meant everyone home.

While the boys were with their Baba, I met a friend at a nightclub.

The music was loud. The lights were low. Nicholas

appeared out of nowhere. His hand closed around me and slammed me into a wall. The crack rang through my skull. Concrete scraped my cheek. Pain burst sharply. The music warped.

Bouncers rushed in. Police lights cut through the dark. He was gone by the time they arrived.

I was back in the hospital. Again. With a concussion.

For three years, it kept going. The pattern had a rhythm by then—not predictable, but familiar. The body learns the shape of a recurring thing even when it cannot prepare for it. I had stopped being surprised. I had not stopped being afraid. Those two things, I was learning, could exist at the same time.

As the pressure built, I knew my children needed relief from survival.

Money was tight. I found a "free" seven-night stay in Florida—payment hidden in a ninety-minute sales pitch I endured for their laughter. I sat in that presentation room and nodded and smiled and watched the clock and thought: this is the price of a week. I can pay this price.

On the beach, the sun pressed warm against our skin. They ran and splashed and shouted, their voices cutting through the air. A tightness loosened—not gone, but loosened. I stood at the waterline and watched them and let myself be, briefly, only a mother at the beach with her boys. Not a woman being hunted. Not a woman counting exits. Just a mother. The ocean did not care about any of the rest of it. It just kept coming in.

Even the accidents couldn't undo it—Adam slipping

under a wave before I hauled him back, coughing and shaking; Ramone splitting his chin on the pool deck, blood bright against the blue water; Samuel's shoulders burning red and blistered. Ramone and Samuel both ended up in the hospital. My fear buzzed low and constant.

Still, the week held.

Each presentation earned us another trip—another brief escape. I watched the clock. I nodded when I was supposed to. I did it because it gave them joy. Miami. Daytona Beach. Hershey Park.

Laughter marked each mile. Their giggles filled the car, rising and falling as we drove. Sticky fingers from cotton candy. Sunburned noses. The smell of salt and sunscreen clung to our clothes long after we were home.

On the drives back, the road hummed beneath us. Ramone counted license plates, calling out the ones from other states. He kept score as if it mattered. It mattered. Everything that was ordinary and childlike and unafraid mattered more than I could say. I drove and listened to him count and thought: this is what I am doing all of it for. This sound, right here. This boy in the back seat with his window down, keeping score.

Sometimes he'd laugh at a silly song on the radio, the sound cutting through the quiet, and I'd hear Baba's voice beneath it—the rhythm of his stories, the particular frequency of his laugh. Baba, who had driven the wrong way and laughed until the horns blurred. Baba, who had said see, life doesn't always have to be rocky. I heard him in those moments from the back seat. I was glad for it. I let him in.

On quieter weekends, I joined a bowling league.

The crash of pins felt final—punctuation at the end of long weeks. Each strike landed clean and certain, the way almost nothing else in my life did. That's where I met Karen, grounded and kind, with laughter that didn't ask permission.

Between frames, we talked. Kids. Work. Aches that didn't go away. Small victories that mattered. We shared fries from the snack bar, hands greasy, stories tumbling out that made us laugh and ache in the same breath. I had not had a friend like that in a long time—someone who did not require an explanation before she sat beside you. Karen just sat.

The first night, I picked up my ball, took my stance, and released it with confidence. The ball shot sideways, hopped the lane divider, and rolled straight into the next lane. A guy two lanes over yelled,

"Ma'am, that's not your lane!"

I stared at the runaway ball like it had betrayed me personally.

"Well," I said, hands on my hips, "it wanted a change of scenery."

Karen lost it.

"Oh my God—your ball's networking."

The bowling attendant jogged over, trying very hard not to smile.

"First night?"

"Is it that obvious?" I asked.

He handed me another ball.

"This one should stay in its lane." He winked.

I rolled it. It went straight. It hit one pin and

stopped.

Karen started laughing. A few people nearby joined her. I bowed anyway.

"Thank you," I said. "I'll be signing autographs after the third gutter."

I have thought about that night many times since. Not because anything important happened. Because nothing important happened. We ate fries and bowled badly and laughed at things that were not serious, and no one was watching the door, and the hour did not cost anything except being there. I had forgotten that hours could be like that. Karen reminded me.

When we stepped into the parking lot, the air was cool and still.

I held my keys between my fingers, scanning shadows before unlocking the car. I had not stopped doing that. I did not know when I would stop. Some habits the body keeps long after the danger has changed shape. I had learned not to fight them. I scanned. I checked. Then I got in.

I noticed, that night, that the scan had gotten shorter. That my hand found the lock faster. That the pause between the dark and the opening door was a little less than it used to be.

That was something.

I got in. I drove home. The road was quiet, and I was on it, and I was going somewhere I had chosen.

That was everything.

Chapter 11

New Ground

"Be strong and courageous.
Do not be afraid or discouraged."
(Joshua 1:9, NIV)

Ten years had passed since I broke the window and climbed out. The boys were growing. So was I.

When the boys weren't with me, the house felt too quiet. I wanted someone beside me.

At work, I handled the ads every day. One of them stayed with me.

Singles.

I circled the ad twice before folding the newspaper, the print smudging where my thumb lingered.

"Just call."

By the time I dialed the number, my fingers were numb, the kitchen clock ticking louder with every ring.

Tysons Corner made sense. Close to the Fairfax Journal. No late drive back to Maryland. I booked the room anyway, gripping the receiver longer than necessary before hanging up.

That night, I drove to a hotel where Maryland and Virginia meet. Traffic rushed past in streaks of light.

Storefronts glowed. The city pressed in on both sides—close enough to sense, distant enough to feel like leaving one life without entering another. I had left lives before. Those leavings had been desperate, through broken windows and across gravel. This one was a choice. I kept reminding myself of that: this is a choice. You are allowed to make it.

In the parking lot, engine idling, I rested my forehead against the steering wheel and waited for the shaking to pass.

I stepped through the hotel doors.

The lighting dimmed. Sound softened to bar chatter and the elevator's hum. The scent of polished wood and waxed floors pulled me back into my body. I ran my fingers along the cool marble counter and felt my breath return. I paused in the lobby, my hand tightening around my purse strap.

Inside the ballroom, people holding drinks too tightly, eyes lifting and dropping, faces searching for something familiar. Laughter surfaced in short bursts, then faded. I watched shoulders square and soften, hands loosen and tighten.

My own shoulders dropped a fraction.

Glasses clinked. Laughter overlapped. A band tuned in the background, close enough to hear the mistakes. Light fractured through the crystal and spilled across the pressed linen and polished shoes. Perfume, cologne, the faint bite of alcohol. My heart beat hard beneath a thrift store dress. The fabric sat wrong on my shoulder. I tightened my grip on the stem of my glass, unsure whether to set it down.

Trust hovered out of reach.

First names only. Ages scribbled in ink.

"Great Expectations."

A woman beside me adjusted her bracelet, metal sliding softly against her wrist. She glanced over.

"You look nervous."

I let out a breath I hadn't realized I was holding.

"Is it that obvious?"

She smiled—not curious, not judging. Just kind.

"First time here? Don't worry. We're all just trying to start over."

Her words rested against me, like a brief hand at my back. Then a laugh broke somewhere behind me. It snapped my body before my mind could catch up. I scanned the room, searching for a sharp voice, a shift in tone. Nothing did. The music kept playing. People leaned closer to one another. The words rose anyway. I moved further into the room, heels tapping lightly, plush carpet swallowing the sound as I searched for a spark without knowing what it would feel like.

I saw Don.

His blue eyes met mine, open, and something in me lifted. His calm smile held. The noise in me eased. I hadn't known that kind of ease in years. I had forgotten it existed—that a room could simply quiet when someone looked at you. That a stranger's face could do that.

"Are those any good?" I asked, nodding toward the salsa and chips.

He smiled and slid the basket closer.

"I don't know. I haven't tried them."

Conversation followed without effort. I told him

about my work at the Fairfax Journal, the long drives between Maryland and Virginia, deadlines that stretched late into the night. He listened, offering pieces of his own life in return, small hopes tucked into the edges of his words. When he spoke, my body didn't brace. When he smiled, I didn't look away. I noticed both of those things. They were not small.

As midnight approached, I invited him to my room. He met my eyes and waited, giving me the space to decide.

In the soft light of a single lamp, he sat beside me, close enough that our shoulders touched. His hand rested on the cushion between us, palm open.

We talked about small things. The drive. The music that had been playing. A story from his day. His voice stayed low, even, unhurried.

He reached once to tuck a loose strand of hair behind my ear, then let his hand fall back to his own lap.

I wasn't used to that—being given room. For years, space had been something taken from me, not offered. Hands had reached without asking, voices had filled rooms without leaving any air for mine. Don's open palm on the cushion between us was such a small thing. I sat with it for a long time after he left. I sat with the fact that a hand could simply rest somewhere and wait, and nothing bad would follow. I was thirty years old and I was learning this for the first time.

Our bond stretched across the distance between Maryland and Virginia.

At the Fairfax Journal, I stayed late, coffee cooling beside my keyboard.

One weekend, Don pressed a key into my palm.

"Use it whenever you need a break."

Centreville was quiet then. The roads narrowed. Fields opened. I sat on his sofa, my shoulders dropped. I had not noticed how rarely my shoulders dropped until they did. The body keeps its own accounts.

The first time I reached into a closet for a towel, I saw them—magazines stacked in the corner. My stomach tightened. I stood there longer than necessary, the towel slipping in my hand.

I waited for Don to come home.

"Don... I need to talk to you."

He met my eyes.

"Of course. Is anything wrong?"

"I was looking for a towel. I found these magazines. They don't feel right here. Not in a life we're building together."

His face tightened, surprise flickering. Then he nodded.

"You're right. They don't belong here anymore."

We carried them out together and dropped them in the bin. No arguing. No explanations. No cost to me for having said the thing.

I stood at the bin for a moment after. I had said what I needed and he had listened and we had done something about it and the world had not ended. I had not been punished. The evening had continued. We went back inside and made dinner and the silence between us was easy and that—that ordinary, unremarkable ease—was something I had not known a relationship could hold.

The rhythm of my days shifted. Mornings began before light. Evenings stretched past dark. I traded the newsroom's ringing phones and humming printers for a law office near the Fairfax courthouse, where heels clicked against tile and files thudded onto polished desks. The walkways filled early and emptied long after sunset. Our schedules fell into step.

His proposal came quietly.

City Hall. No crowd. No speeches. We signed the papers, stood close, and walked back out with our hands still joined.

We were married on November 30, 1994. Quietly. Without ceremony.

Bare branches scraped the sky as autumn thinned into winter.

Don followed me to Maryland to help me pack. He lifted boxes without asking what was fragile, waited when I paused, and held doors as pieces of the past surfaced and passed. When everything was loaded, we drove back together and unlocked the door to his place. I stood in the doorway for a moment before I crossed it. There had been so many thresholds. So many doors that had opened into something I did not choose. I chose this one.

Our Golden Oak condo came alive—shoes lining the wall, backpacks by the door, voices where silence used to sit.

The boys—eight, nine, and ten—walked into new classrooms, their shoulders stiffening week by week.

Bikes tipped into the grass outside. Windows stood open. Mornings became cereal bowls, juice boxes crinkling, papers sliding across the table.

Don leaned over Samuel's homework, pencil tapping once, then still.

"Step by step."

"You're smarter than this."

Ramone nudged his brother.

"Not that hard."

On Saturdays, Don took the boys to a shelter in Fairfax. They stood shoulder to shoulder, aprons tied too loose, ladling soup, wiping tables.

"Just smile," Don told Ramone, guiding his hand.

Samuel giggled as he passed out pastries.

"Felt bad for the homeless, Mom," Ramone said later.

Hearing him, I thought of Ramallah—plates passed, doors left open, no one turned away. Yamma's hands moving food toward whoever needed it. The baker who said for Um Ibrahim, never. Something was being passed down, even here, even in a Fairfax shelter with aprons tied too loose. The thread held.

A year later, beneath the bathroom light, the test strip darkened.

Pink bloomed, unmistakable.

"A baby?" Don said, a smile breaking through.

The word lifted, then hung there. My thoughts moved ahead—ribbons, softer laughter, a different weight in my arms. At night, I let the questions pass—faith, discipline, who she might become.

The pregnancy pressed hard. Bed rest. IV drips. Nurses moved in and out.

She will be worth it.

Before the contractions took hold, the news flickered on—a woman delivering in an ambulance, snow closing the roads behind her. I held still. The roads were disappearing, tires cutting slow paths through snow that kept falling. Don kept both hands steady on the wheel, easing forward, careful, even as my contractions tightened.

She arrived during the blizzard of 1996, snow clawing at the hospital windows, wind rattling the glass like it wanted in.

Her weight was warm and certain in my arms. Her curls were thick and black, tightly wound, a small crown.

This baby can't be mine.

Not because she didn't look like me—because she looked untouched. Spared. The boys had arrived in crisis—early, bruised by the conditions of their coming, each one entering the world in the middle of something that should not have been happening. This child had arrived in a blizzard, yes, but a blizzard is just weather. It doesn't mean you. She had been sheltered inside a body that, for the first time in years, had not been afraid every day. I looked at her face and thought: you got the version of me that was becoming safe. You came in at the right time. I am glad you got that. I am so glad you got that.

Snow piled against the windows. The blizzard sealed the room—warm air, beeping machines, the sharp scent of clean sheets and hospital soap.

The door swung open, and the boys hurried in, cheeks red, voices rushing as they gathered close. They claimed her without hesitation.

"She's so tiny," Adam whispered.

Ramone leaned in, breathing her in.

Samuel giggled when her curled fingers closed around his.

They took turns holding her, arguing softly over who rocked her best. I watched them—these three boys who had been through everything I had been through, who had slept in basements and fled through windows and sat in courthouse hallways with their legs swinging—holding their sister like she was the most ordinary miracle. Which she was. Which they all were. I had not always been able to see that. Standing in that hospital room in the middle of a blizzard, I saw it clearly.

Three days later, we went home.

Two weeks after that, the crying began—not fussing, relentless, the kind that thins nights and frays nerves.

It pulled me back to Ramone—the same sharp, unending cry.

"Please stop."

"What am I doing wrong?" Kissing her damp forehead.

Ms. Frances, our next-door neighbor, took Jodie into her arms and rocked her with hands that never rushed. To the kids, she became Teta. Fatigue, in layers.

Ramone kept pulling me upright.

"She's smiling!" Ramone shouted, hope breaking

through exhaustion.

Darkness hovered. Ramone stayed close.

"It's okay, Mama. I got you."

I thought about the incubator. Two pounds. The nurse who said he can't come home until he reaches five pounds. The nights I had stood with my finger against the warm plastic and said just keep breathing, habibi. I had counted his breaths then so he would keep taking them.

Now he was standing beside me in the dark, making sure I kept taking mine. Ramone, who had come into the world fighting, was still fighting—only now he was fighting for me.

I held that. I did not let it go.

His laughter carried me through.

I hadn't spoken to my family in fifteen years—not until Jodie was born.

It took me days to dial the number. I set the phone down, picked it up again. When I finally called, my voice sounded unfamiliar in my own ears. Fifteen years is a long time to be without the people who first said your name. It is also a long time to need them and not call. Both things were true. I had needed them. I had not called. The silence had been protection, and it had been loss at the same time. Dialing that number meant admitting both.

On the drive to New Jersey, the kids sensed the shift before I said a word.

"Mom, are you okay?" Adam asked from the backseat.

"I'm fine."

Ramone leaned forward.

"Are they going to like us?"

"They'll love you. They just haven't seen us in a long time."

Samuel glanced at his sister asleep in her car seat.

"Do they know about Jodie?"

"They know. They'll meet all of you today."

The road stretched ahead, gray and familiar, tugging low. We drove north in silence, each mile bringing its own unease.

When we arrived, Yamma wrapped her arms around me and my children one by one. Her face lit up. She cupped my cheeks, her hands warm, her eyes wet, affection delivered without words after all those years. The hands I had watched my whole life—folding grape leaves, smoothing embroidery, pressing a paper towel into a frightened girl's palm—cupped my face now as if I were still that girl. I let her hold me there. I did not pull away.

"Hala, kefik, how are you?"

"I'm fine."

"My children wanted to meet you."

Ikhwani gathered close, voices overlapping, teasing and questions, the sound of childhood returning all at once. They studied my children, smiling at the years they hadn't seen. Yamma cupped her hands to their faces and whispered,

"Subhan Allah—glory be to God—they look just like you."

Fifteen years folded in on themselves.

Ibrahim stepped forward and pulled me into an embrace, his grip firm, his shoulders tight. He held on longer than I expected. I felt in his grip what he was not yet saying—the weight of it, the years of it, the thing he had been carrying since the kitchen in Ramallah when he stood silent and became part of the sentence.

"I'm sorry you didn't get to come to Baba's funeral."

"I wanted to be there."

"Nicholas forbade it."

He nodded. The moment held.

"I know you've been wanting to go back home."

"I'll fly you and the kids and take care of everything."

Days later, he returned with plane tickets in his hand.

"Take the kids."

"Go visit Baba."

I took the tickets. I held them the way Baba used to hold letters—smoothing the fold, running a thumb along the edge, as if the paper itself had something to say. All those years I had carried the not-going. The red earth I never stood beside. The goodbye said only to a photograph. Ibrahim was handing me back something I had thought was gone permanently. There are debts that cannot be repaid. And then sometimes, unexpectedly, someone tries. I let him try. I folded the tickets carefully and put them somewhere safe.

We were going to Jerusalem.

We were going to Baba.

Chapter 12

ROOTS RECLAIMED

"I will restore to you the years the locusts have eaten."
(Joel 2:25, NIV)

In the five-hour drive back to Virginia, the road rumbled beneath us. Headlights stretched into the dark, one after another, disappearing behind us. The boys replayed the visit in bursts—voices overlapping, rising and falling—as the miles slipped by.

"Mama, did you see Ibrahim cry?" Adam asked. "He never cries."

"He missed you," I said. "All of us did."

Ramone kicked his sneakers against the back of my seat.

"I liked her. She smelled like soap and bread."

I laughed softly. "She'll be happy to hear that."

Samuel leaned forward between the seats.

"Does she always kiss your cheeks like that?"

"That's how she shows love."

Their voices rose and fell with the road, filling the car until the ache loosened its grip and the miles carried us home. By the time we pulled into Virginia, the boys had grown quiet. The visit had done something to them I couldn't fully name yet—something that settles slowly, like sediment. They had touched something that belonged to them before they were born. They would not understand it for years. But it was in them now.

Back home, I told Don about the trip—the laughter, the tears that came too late, Ibrahim's arms around me, the plane tickets pressed into my hand. He sat at the table and listened, nodding once in a while, letting my words settle between us.

"It felt like healing."

I looked around our kitchen—tight corners, chipped cabinets, Jodie's bottle drying by the sink. The walls pressed closer than I remembered.

Teta's kitchen rose without warning—olives slick with oil, eggplant cooling on metal trays, her voice calling us in. The smell lingered—sharp, familiar.

If we're going to be gone for a few weeks, I thought, my fingers resting on the counter, this is the moment. The idea wouldn't let go.

I started calling contractors, flipping through numbers until Don mentioned someone from his work—a coworker's husband who remodeled homes. Two days later, I sat across from him at our kitchen table, papers spread wide, corners curling.

"It needs to be finished before we return."

He nodded, pencil hovering over the plans. His boot shifted. Sawdust clung to the leather. Plaster dust clung to his sleeves.

"I'll do my best."

The pencil tapped once, then stilled. I gathered the papers, squared the stack, and stood. As I pulled the front door closed behind me, a fine cloud of dust slipped from the ceiling and settled onto the floor, caught the light, then disappeared. I noted it without knowing why. The body sometimes notices what the mind is not ready to.

I packed our bags. Locked the door. For a moment, I stood outside, the key still in my hand, before turning away.

Don drove us to the airport.

I'm coming home, Baba.

At Dulles, the terminal pulsed with departures—rolling suitcases, boarding calls stacking over one another, voices rising and falling like waves. Backpacks bulged with crayons and snacks.

"How big is the plane, Mama?"

"Do they have food?"

For years, missing Baba's funeral had lived in me like an open wound. Nicholas's refusal had cut a vital tether loose, forcing the ache into silence. I had carried the not-going the way you carry something you are not allowed to put down—invisibly, constantly, until the weight becomes indistinguishable from your own body. Walking through those departure doors, I felt it shift. Not lift. Shift. As if it had finally agreed to move with me rather than against me.

Seatbelts clicked as the plane began to move. Overhead bins thudded shut. A child laughed behind me, sharp and unbothered. As the wheels lifted from the runway, something tightened in me—not from the altitude, but from where I was going.

Home. At last.

We boarded the flight to London and settled into our seats, the boys whispering and giggling, leaning toward the windows. The cabin air dried my throat. That familiar long-flight stillness closed in.

They pressed their faces to the glass, pointing at clouds stretched wide beneath us.

"They look like cotton," one of them said.

Their voices pulled me backward—1973. A little girl with her forehead against a plane window, drawing a house in the corner of a page with a blue crayon, leaving the rest white. I had called those clouds winter. My boys renamed them in wonder. The same sky. Different children. The same distance crossed, but this time forward instead of away.

Their excitement steadied me as the ocean opened below, blue water spreading wide like something without end.

Midway through the flight, a flight attendant bent toward us.

"Would your boys like to see the cockpit?"

We followed her past the curtain, the narrow aisle, the quiet choreography of hands and switches—attendants moving with the same calm grace I remembered from that first flight, when a woman with kind eyes had pressed crayons into my small hands. A kindness I hadn't known how to name then. I knew now. It was the same thing: someone looking at a child in transit and deciding to give her something beautiful to do with her hands.

The cockpit glowed. Buttons blinked. Screens traced

thin green lines across oceans and continents.

"Can we touch anything?" Adam whispered.

The captain smiled and pointed to a harmless button. "Just this one."

Amber light blinked beneath Adam's fingertip. The boys inhaled together. Awe widened their faces.

I stood behind them, my hands resting lightly on their shoulders, and understood something I had not been able to articulate before that moment: I had not brought them here to see where I came from. I had brought them here so they would know that they came from somewhere. That there was a place before the basements, before the broken windows, before the courthouse hallways. That their roots ran deeper than any of that. That they were not only what had happened to them. They were also this—these olive trees, these limestone walls, this sky, this cockpit light blinking amber under a small hand that carried all of it forward.

The plane hummed around us, carrying us toward what was waiting.

Heathrow opened around us in chorus—wheels rattling over tile, voices lifting and falling, coffee and cinnamon drifting through the air.

In the restroom shuffle, Jodie heavy on my hip, bags dragging at my wrists, I reached for my purse.

My hand closed on nothing.

I checked again. Slower this time. Then faster.

Gone. Our passports. Our money. Our way forward.

Jodie let out a sharp cry, startled by the shift in my

body. The boys stepped closer, eyes widening as they watched my face change.

"Mama... what's wrong?"

"My purse... I lost it."

Something locked inside me. My hands went cold. The sink, the mirrors, the hard white tile—everything blurred. The airport surged with noise—babies crying, luggage wheels clattering, voices colliding. All I could hear was my pulse. Loud. Fast. Unforgiving.

The boys watched me closely, waiting for the steadiness I always gave them.

I had none.

Then the speaker crackled overhead.

"Halaina Thinnes, please come to airport security."

Someone had turned it in. Everything intact.

My knees gave out before I could thank her. Gratitude came out broken—not elegant, not composed. Just real. I had learned, over the years, to receive grace without trying to make it smaller than it was. Someone had found our passports and turned them in. Someone had made it possible for us to keep going. I stood in that airport and let myself feel the full size of that.

We gathered ourselves and moved on.

By the time we boarded, the kids settled into their seats, excitement fading into sleep. Their bodies felt warm against mine. I stayed awake, watching the dark horizon stretch beneath the wing, feeling the pull of home grow heavier with each mile.

"Ramallah," I whispered as we descended into Ben-

Gurion, Tel Aviv glowing beneath us.

Lights scattered across the earth like shaken gold dust. As the coastline curved into view, recognition settled in my chest—quiet, but certain. The boys pressed their faces to the window, searching for what I felt in my bones.

I wasn't just visiting. I was arriving in my past.

At baggage claim, Khalati Tamam and Jamila rushed toward us, tears spilling before words, their arms wrapping around me—years folding into a single moment.

"Ya rohi, my soul."

"Ya zaman, it has been so long," Tamam cried.

We spent those days in Ibrahim's condo—whitewashed walls, balcony herbs, an iron door that sighed with age. Each day, we visited relatives; dishes arrived seasoned with stories.

Mansaf sat at the center of the table—lamb and rice soaked in jameed, its sharp, fermented tang tying everything together. Earthy. Ancient.

Adam took the first bite and froze.

"Mama... why does it taste like this?"

Ramone leaned in, sniffing the lamb.

"It smells strong."

Tamam laughed. "It's supposed to make you strong."

Adam chewed again. "Okay... this is actually good."

Ramone nodded. "Better than chicken nuggets."

Laughter moved around the table. No one rushed it.

For a moment, the boys weren't visitors. They were home. They didn't know it yet—but their bodies did. I watched them settle into the noise and the food and the hands reaching for them across the table, and I thought: this is what I wanted to give them. Not a lesson. This feeling. This belonging to something larger than what had happened to us.

Ramallah blurred between past and present. Children darted between carts; women sold vegetables from cloth-lined baskets. The city moved with its own rhythm—stubborn, alive.

I told the boys about Maha's laughter, about our races through these alleys. We wandered down memory's lane—streets where Maha chased me, doorways where Yamma called us home, stone paths worn smooth by generations.

Harat al-Nasarah opened before us—laundry strung between balconies, a neighbor pouring water down the steps, the scent of soap drifting through warm air. A boy kicked a dented soccer ball, the thud echoing the rhythm of my childhood.

Just beyond the curve stood my old house. Smaller than memory, still standing.

The new owners welcomed us with coffee and biscuits—genuine Ramallah hospitality. I touched the familiar wall. The cool surface steadied my breathing.

"We lived here when I was little... I'd forgotten how small it was."

Tears came fast. I didn't stop them. I could almost hear Yamma's footsteps, feel the kanun warming our legs, hear her stories drifting through the dawn. The house was smaller than I remembered and larger than I had let myself imagine in all the years I stayed away. Both things were true. Memory does that—it both shrinks and expands a place, depending on how long you have been gone from it.

The boys tried to imagine twelve people living in two rooms.

We stepped outside and continued to Ghanem Street—its stones uneven, the old fig tree leaning over the wall, casting crooked shadows.

"This is Ghanem Street," I said.

I pictured my younger self darting ahead, Maha beside me, sandals slapping stone as we chased the evening call to prayer. Maha, who had named clouds from a rooftop. Maha, who had said don't cry, and whom I had never stopped missing, not for a single day. I walked her street with her nephews and let her be present in the only way she still could be.

At the bend, Aziz Shaheen appeared—unchanged in its bones. Children ran across the dusty yard where Maha and I once raced, laughter rising into the warm air.

We walked to the church where Ibrahim got married. The stone still held the hush of that day—the lace dress itching my arms, Maha's proud smile glowing in memory.

El-Manara opened before us—its five lions keeping watch as always.

"Did you climb them, Mama?"

"No. I once felt them."

I thought of Yamma's hand over mine against the cool stone. They don't forget, she had said. I had not forgotten. I pressed my palm to the nearest lion and held it there. The stone was warm now, not cool. The city had been breathing on it all morning.

The boys ran ahead, laughter lifting into the square. Ramallah stretched its arms around them the way it once did for me.

As vendors shouted their prices, Adam tugged my sleeve.

"Why do they shout like that?"

"They want everyone to hear them. That's how they sell."

Ramone pointed to a grape seller.

"He sounds mad."

"He's not. He wants passersby to know his grapes are sweet."

By afternoon, we reached Ibrahim's courtyard. Khalati poured thick, fragrant coffee. We talked quietly about neighbors who'd left, families who'd returned, and the way time folds and unfolds in a place like this.

"You've carried so much," she said softly. "Look how God brought you back... with your children."

Then a scream sliced the calm.

A rock thrown by nearby children had struck Adam.

We ran to Al-Hussein Hospital—dim corridors, sour air beneath the disinfectant, floors marked with what had come before. People leaned against the walls—coughing children, a woman pressing a cloth to her forehead, an old man slumped in a chair.

"He's going to need one stitch," the nurse said.

Adam didn't cry.

"I'm okay, Mama."

His hand held mine. I looked at him—this boy who had been born eight months into a life of violence, who had screamed stop hurting Mommy from a room I couldn't reach. Now he was holding my hand to steady me. The inversion was not lost on me. It never was.

Afterward, we stepped into the warm air. I told him scars were stories—marks of bravery.

We stopped for sticky knafeh and warm tea. Their laughter returned, soft with relief.

By morning, we were ready to keep going.

Jerusalem rose before us in layers of stone and sun.

The air thickened as we climbed—warmer, heavier, carrying dust and history in equal measure. Light struck the walls at sharp angles, turning stone gold, then blinding white.

Damascus Gate swallowed us whole. Sound hit first—voices colliding, carts rattling over uneven ground.

I took a breath.

Then the rest came—color, heat, the press of bodies.

"Five shekels! Five shekels!"

A vendor snapped a shirt through the air. The sound stopped me cold.

I wasn't a woman walking with children.

I was small again—my hand swallowed in someone else's palm. This was my childhood. I searched faces without meaning to, my body remembering before my mind caught up.

Around us, the crowd surged.

Then I saw them.

Khalati, Nahme, Musadey, and Amo Samir stood beyond the gate, exactly where they said they would be. Older now, lines etched deeper, but unmistakable. Faces carried forward from summers long past, from visits stitched into my youth.

For a moment, none of us moved.

Then arms opened.

Years folded inward as they pulled me close, their hands firm, grounding me back into my body. Around us, the clatter of footsteps and voices continued, but inside that circle, everything stilled. And I stood there—held between who I had been and who I had become—knowing this city wasn't welcoming me.

It already knew me.

Nearly thirty cracked stone steps climbed toward Denise's house, their worn surfaces slick beneath our feet. By the time we reached the top, the afternoon light had begun to thin, sliding across the walls in long bands of gold.

The adhan rose across the rooftops, stretching and folding into itself as it traveled. Inside, mint clung faintly to the air, mixed with the dry sweetness of old wood. A fan turned lazily in the corner, its hum punctuated by the distant toll of church bells slipping through half-open shutters.

The city pressed beyond the walls. Everything slowed.

Below us, Jerusalem moved. Heat lifted from the streets in visible waves. Fabric stalls rippled as vendors shook their wares. Skewers hissed over open flames.

Spice drifted upward—shawarma fat dripping onto flame, khubz pulled hot from ovens.

The city announced itself in scent, heat, and motion.

I had grown up with the adhan and the church bells braiding through the same window. My boys had grown up with neither. Standing on that rooftop, I watched them hear both at once—not competing, not explaining themselves, simply rising into the same air—and I saw something move across their faces that I could not name but recognized. The beginning of understanding that the world is larger and older and more layered than the streets they had grown up on. That was enough. That was everything I had come to give them.

At the Church of the Holy Sepulcher, cool air wrapped around us—incense, candle smoke, stone. The moment we crossed the threshold, the city fell away.

Light dimmed into an amber hush. Pilgrims moved through the shadows—languages overlapping, scarves brushing shoulders, footsteps slowing under the weight of reverence. Ancient arches loomed overhead, their darkened stone holding centuries of flame and prayer.

The boys fell silent. Their eyes followed the tremble of candlelight along the walls. Each footstep echoed—hollow, deliberate. Faith didn't need words here.

We climbed the limestone steps, worn smooth by generations, slick beneath our shoes. At the top, the Virgin Mary stood behind glass, her robe edged in gold, candlelight catching across her face.

"This is the Virgin Mary," I said softly. "People come

from everywhere to see her."

Ramone leaned closer. "Why behind glass?"

"To protect her. She's very sacred."

The boys stared up at her, gold softly reflecting across their faces, awe settling over them into holy stillness.

Adam touched the Stone of Anointing.

"Is this really where Jesus was laid?"

"It is."

He pressed his hand to the stone. Time seemed to pause beneath his palm. I watched him stand there—this boy who had been born into chaos, who had placed his small hand on his mother's shoulder in a courthouse hallway, who had learned too early that the world could be violent and unfair—pressing his palm to the oldest grief in the world. Something passed through him. I could see it. I did not interrupt it.

Outside, the city returned all at once—voices rising, footsteps quickening, the hum of movement pulling us back into it.

The courtyard at the Church of All Nations held an older stillness. Olive trees twisted upward, their trunks thick and gnarled, roots gripping the earth.

Light filtered through the leaves in narrow strands, shifting as the branches moved. Pilgrims stood in quiet pockets—some touching the bark, others whispering prayers.

The boys slowed without me asking, drawn into the hush.

"Mama... is this where He prayed?"

"Yes. This is the Garden of Gethsemane."

Ramone studied plaques engraved with the Lord's Prayer in different languages.

"Why so many prayers?"

"It's one prayer," I said. "Written in everyone's language."

He stood with that for a long moment. I let him.

At the Western Wall, the crowd pressed close, softening into a hush. Men leaned into the stone, foreheads resting against its warmth. Some rocked gently as they prayed. Others stood still, lips moving silently. Folded papers slipped into the cracks, fingers lingering as if reluctant to let go.

The boys stepped forward and placed their hands on the wall.

"It's hot," Adam whispered.

"It's been holding prayers for thousands of years."

Ramone leaned closer, studying the papers tucked between the stones.

"Mama... why do they put papers in the wall?"

"Each one is a prayer."

He nodded, slowly. Then he reached into his pocket, found a scrap of paper, and folded it small. He pressed it into a crack. He did not tell me what he had written. I did not ask. Some prayers are between a person and the stone.

We stepped back into the street. A falafel cart sizzled at the corner, oil popping as the vendor flipped the rounds. The smell pulled us forward. We ate standing up, fingers slick, heat warming our palms as traffic and voices folded around us, my boys beside me, whole.

Cypress trees stood at the gate of Oscar Schindler's cemetery, tall and watchful, their needles shifting softly in the breeze.

"Mama... why rocks and not flowers?"

"Rocks stay," I said. "Flowers fade."

Schindler's grave lay covered in stones—hands had been here before ours, thousands of them. Adam traced a name with his finger. Ramone bent and placed a pebble carefully among the others.

"Why so many stones, Mama?"

"He's never forgotten."

My feet carried me farther in.

Toward Baba.

His resting place appeared simple at first—a rectangle of stone, Arabic letters carved with care, weeds pushing up through the earth. Time had worn the edges smooth, but his name was still there. The name I had been carrying since the carpet store phone call. Since the photograph with the corners worn soft from handling. Since the letter folded and folded again at the kitchen table.

I knelt.

The moment my knees touched the ground, I broke.

"Mama?" Ramone whispered. "Why are you crying like that?"

Adam stepped closer, his small hand resting on my shoulder.

"It's okay, Mama. We're here."

I pressed my palms to the stone, cool beneath my hands. I closed my eyes. For a moment, I felt what I had always needed to feel in this place: that he knew I had come. That the distance between his death and this moment—all the years I had been kept from standing here, all the grief I had carried in photographs and folded letters—had finally, today, been closed.

The wind shifted, lifting the hair at my temples.

Baba, who had driven the wrong way down a one-way street and laughed until the horns blurred. Baba, who had pressed his palm to a page and said you'll get there. Baba, who had been beside me, never in front of what ruled. Baba, who had not lived to see what ruled finally ended.

I wanted him to know.

"This is Jiddo... your grandfather," I told them. "My Baba. I didn't get to say goodbye."

The boys knelt and each chose a small stone. They placed them gently on the grave.

"For him," they said.

"I miss you," I whispered. "I finally made it, Baba."

The wind shifted again. Somewhere, a church bell rang—soft and familiar. The same bell that had braided with the adhan through every window of my childhood. I let it ring. I let it be enough.

My sobs eased. I stayed a moment longer, my hands on his stone, my children around me. Then I stood.

The world stirred around us.

"Kaak! Kaak hami! Hot sesame bread!"

The call carried the same way it had when I was a child. The scent wrapped around us. Life moved on. I didn't—not right away. I pulled the boys close.

"Come," I whispered.

"Let's go home."

Back at my Khalati's house in Jerusalem, cardamom coffee softened the day. Evening gathered slowly, stories drifting between cups, voices low and unhurried.

A neighbor slipped in for coffee readings, her voice steady as she traced shapes in the dark grounds, speaking softly as if the future required gentleness. I watched her turn the cup and thought of all the women in Ramallah who had done this—tracing the future in what was left behind. I had believed in it as a child. I believed in it still. Not because it was certain, but because it was a way of sitting together and saying: we are still here, and the future is still possible, and we will look at it together.

The next morning, a family friend invited us to a baptism.

Bethlehem glowed honey-gold in the afternoon light. Shops spilled rosaries onto narrow shelves; vendors called softly, their voices folding into the rhythm of the street. Spices warmed the air.

We walked toward the Church of the Nativity, its stone walls rising above the crowd, holding everything in a quiet suspension. Centuries pressed close. Light dimmed. Candles flickered.

Greek Orthodox families filled the church, then spilled beneath a large tent stretched tight in the afternoon light. Candles were pressed into small hands. White garments were laid out with care.

We had come as witnesses. But something shifted.

One by one, families stepped forward and claimed my children. They offered to stand as godparents—four families, one for each child. They covered everything: the church, the clothes, the ceremony, the meals afterward. No one asked. It was done with open hands.

I thought of Ibrahim's voice—visit Baba and baptize the kids—and felt the moment drawing closer.

"Mama... is this really where He was born?"

"Yes. Here."

We descended into the lower chamber. Silver lamps hung overhead. Incense thickened the air, prayers murmured in layers—old, unbroken. Beneath our feet, a large silver star was set into the stone, marking the place of His birth. Around it, the words were carved: Hic de Virgine Maria Jesus Christus natus est—Here Jesus Christ was born of the Virgin Mary.

Beeswax candles burned slowly, wax pooling in soft amber at their base.

The boys stood in their suits, solemn and still. Jodie wore white.

The priest's voice rose and fell. Oil gleamed on skin. Water caught the light.

Adam and Ramone were immersed—three gentle dips each—the water moving across their faces.

Jodie trembled in the priest's hands, tiny and luminous, her cry brief before settling into stillness.

I had delivered Adam alone in a hospital with bruises the nurses noticed but did not press. I had held Ramone through an incubator for months before I could bring him home. I had bought one-way tickets to New Jersey with stolen money and Samuel had arrived in the chaos of the running. They had all come into the world in crisis, in violence, in flight. Every birth marked by something that should not have been happening.

This time, they were mine to witness. All of them, here, in the oldest light in the world, surrounded by people who had stepped forward with open hands and said: we claim these children. We will stand for them.

No one had ever stood for them like that before.

I had no words. I stood in the candlelight and let it be wordless.

Rice and rose petals fell, brushing our shoulders.

Across the square, the adhan rose. Church bells answered. Two voices lifting into the same sky.

Two days later, Jodie burned with fever.

The neighbor arrived at the sound of my voice, sleeves rolled. She filled a basin with cool water, murmuring old remedies as she worked—words soft and rhythmic, like prayers released into the air. Jodie whimpered, then stilled.

I stayed beside her, my hand resting on her small back, counting the rise and fall beneath my palm while the room held its quiet. I had counted breaths before—Maha's, in the dark. Ramone's, through the incubator glass. My own, on a bench at a bus stop in the middle of a decision I almost didn't pull back from. I knew how to count. I counted now.

By morning, the fever broke. Jodie's cheeks flushed softly with returning warmth.

The room exhaled.

Our final week in Ramallah passed gently. Evenings stretched long beneath open skies, voices rising and falling without urgency.

"You were always fearless," Jamila said, smiling through the ache.

I did not correct her. Fearless was not the word. The word was: kept going anyway. But some things are too long to say at the end of an evening, so you accept the shorter version and carry what you know.

Goodbyes cut deep. "Come back," they whispered.

I carried the weight of it with me all the way home to Virginia.

Home was not gentle.

I had left to spare the children the dust, the tearing down.

I came back to absence.

Dust hung in the air. I stepped inside. Cabinets were gone. The space where the stove had been sat open and hollow. The condo stood stripped and hollowed, drywall grit floating through the light like ash.

I stopped in the doorway, Jodie warm against my hip. Our footsteps echoed where a kitchen had been. I tried to remember what it looked like before.

Exposed wires hung from the walls. Bare studs. Nothing finished.

This wasn't what we left.

"How could this happen?"

My voice didn't sound like mine.

The silence answered.

"I trusted the contractor," Don said. He didn't look at me.

I didn't respond. There was nothing to say that the room hadn't already said. I had just stood at my father's grave in Jerusalem. I had watched my children baptized in the oldest church in the world. I had come home to exposed wires and a missing kitchen and a man who wouldn't meet my eyes.

Jodie shifted in my arms, heavy and warm. I tightened my hold on her.

Whatever came next, I would face it. I had done harder things. I had done the hardest things. A stripped kitchen was just a kitchen. It could be rebuilt. I knew, by now, what could not be rebuilt and what could. I knew the difference between rubble and a beginning.

This was a beginning.

I took him to court.

I listened as they read it out.

I won.

I hired someone new. I was there when the contractor walked in—standing in my own doorway, in my own home, with my name on the papers and my children behind me.

I had been in many doorways. I had hidden behind dresses and pressed my face into sweaters and gripped door frames and stood in the dark listening for footsteps. I had been pulled through doorways and pushed out of them and fled through windows when the doors were locked.

This doorway was mine.
I stood in it and did not move aside.

Chapter 13

Dandelion Dreams

"See, I am doing a new thing!
Do you not perceive it?"
(Isaiah 43:19, NIV)

Light stretched across the gleaming kitchen—fresh paint, bright tiles, appliances humming like they'd been there forever. It warmed the steam curling off my mug of Folgers. I didn't drink it. I stood there, expecting something to go wrong.

Nothing did.

I filled in the first line, then stopped. Checked the box. Unchecked it. Then checked it again. My hand ached from the grip I didn't realize I had. I slowed my breath until it matched the hum of the refrigerator—the only sound breaking the silence. I had learned, over the years, to use the refrigerator's hum the way I had once used Maha's breathing—as proof that something steady was still running, that the room was safe, that I could continue.

Line by line, I kept going—not because I trusted it. Because I didn't yet.

ARS Publications.

I wrote the name slowly, letter by letter, the pen pausing between strokes. The ink sank into the paper—dark, deliberate.

Adam.

Ramone.

Samuel.

Their initials followed, firm this time. Not loose. Not scattered. Anchored. I leaned back and pressed my palm against my ribs until the tightness loosened. My breath came shallow, then deepened. The name didn't shift. It held where I'd put it—black ink. No erasing. No backspace.

This wasn't a thought anymore. It existed.

Sunlight scattered across the kitchen, catching the edges of the plastic as I followed the line of her arm—bright for a moment, then softening back into color.

Her hands moved—confident, unafraid.

In that ordinary light—the hum of appliances, the soft thud beneath her hands—a thought formed.

Jodie looked up at me, squealing, lifting a block into the glow like proof.

"I see you, my girl," I said.

"You're building something beautiful."

The words landed heavier than I'd expected. She was building with the unself-conscious certainty of a child who has never been told she is taking up too much space. I had spent years learning how to move through rooms without disturbing them. She moved through rooms like she owned them. I wanted to watch her do that for the rest of my life.

Ramallah returned in fragments—grit on my shoes, prayers whispered so softly they barely counted as sound, the way my back always straightened when I stood at a counter, working, waiting. Old habits lived in the body long after the rooms did. The clean lines. The calm. I lingered.

My fingers moved to the keyboard automatically. Muscle memory took over. Deadlines flickered through my mind, ticking like they always did—an invisible metronome I couldn't turn off.

Johnson's Baby Powder softened the air, turning it almost fragile. Jodie's giggles broke loose near my feet, light and sudden, rising through me.

Jodie reached for the keyboard and tapped a key, pleased with herself.

"Mama, I helped!"

"You sure did," I whispered, even as it filled with symbols I didn't recognize.

I didn't rush to fix it.

The kitchen table surrendered, turning into my desk—our shared territory. Toys spilled across it like evidence of joy. Crayons snapped in half, their waxy sweetness rising warm and familiar. Finger paints dried stiff in their cups. Printer proofs fanned out beneath the open window. Ink hung sharp in the air, softened by the citrus from Jodie's sippy cup and the faint bite of marker.

I sat there, the screen glowing steadily. Jodie click-clacked at the keyboard again, delighted by the sound more than the screen.

"Look at the colors," I said, tilting the laptop toward her.

Outside, school buses groaned along the street, their brakes sighing, doors folding open and shut.

What if I could do this alone? The thought didn't leave. I had thought it before in other forms—standing at the diner counter, selling ads at the Fairfax Journal, signing papers with a wired jaw. What if. I had been asking that question my whole life. The difference was that now, when I asked it, I did not follow it immediately with: but what if it goes wrong. I let it sit by itself. I let it just be a question with a possible yes on the other side.

Bills waited in a neat stack nearby. The newspaper lay open beside me, its headlines bleeding into one another until they blurred. Coffee cooled in my mug, turning flat. The ink smelled sharp, almost sour, mixing with the faint vanilla on Jodie's lotion-warmed cheeks.

I let myself picture it—mornings without rushing, afternoons where work and home moved together instead of pulling apart, a rhythm shaped to the life we were building.

"What if the clients disappear?" I whispered, not brave enough to say it out loud.

Jodie looked up at the sound of my voice.

"Mama?"

"Nothing, baby," I said, smiling.

The newsroom rose in my memory—laughter over vending-machine coffee that tasted faintly burnt, keyboards clacking in overlapping rhythms like a collective pulse. Newsprint lingered there, warm and stale, pages passed hand to hand.

Fairfax had been my classroom—proof that I could learn, earn, and build without needing a degree to recognize my competence. Mrs. Smith had said you're doing so well, Hala, keep practicing. Nancy had firmed my handshake and squared my shoulders. Mike had slid a paper across the counter and said you've been steady. I had been collecting those words for years without knowing I was building something with them.

In its wobbling balance, faces surfaced: Adam's gap-toothed grin, Ramone's quick spark of mischief, Samuel's steady, watchful eyes.

"I can do this," I whispered—claiming the words.

I used to wait for someone else to decide. Now, I leaned in. For the first time, I didn't step back.

Beside me, Jodie's blocks collapsed in bright, joyful ruin.

I folded the paper. I slipped it into my purse and zipped it closed. My resignation letter pressed flat against my side—fresh ink, fresh fear, fresh freedom.

The office looked the same as it always had. But it no longer fit. The cubicle felt small—a box where air thinned and dreams learned to stay quiet. I walked past it slowly, my heels clicking against the carpet. The smell of paper and old coffee clung to the walls. Now it closed in as if my body had finally grown too large for the space. I had spent years making myself smaller. I was done with that particular skill.

"Are you really doing this?" a coworker asked,

leaning over the divider.

"It's time," I said. The words came out firmer than I felt.

"You'll be amazing," she whispered. "Just don't forget us when you're famous."

I smiled, the kind that holds gratitude and grief. Both were there. I had learned not to choose between them.

The office hummed on—phones ringing, keyboards tapping, chairs rolling back and forth—the sound drifting away behind me as I walked toward the door.

That same week, I launched ARS Publications from the kitchen table—a quiet tribute to my three sons. Adam. Ramone. Samuel. Their initials on a letterhead. Their names on something that would outlast the years that had tried to undo us.

I sketched the logo on a napkin amid cereal crumbs—a blooming tree threaded through their initials. Roots sinking deep. Branches reaching.

Success meant bedtime stories and school events I wouldn't miss. It meant being there when the bus pulled up. It meant the particular joy of being the person they looked for first.

While the boys were at school, Jodie and I reshaped the house into a working space. She perched at the old desktop, the WordPerfect icon blinking like a tired eye. Her small hand reached for the keyboard, tapping keys. I leaned down and kissed the top of her head.

"That's beautiful."

She beamed, cheeks caught in the monitor's glare.

Taking her to meetings became my secret joy. She sat beside me in cafés and conference rooms, her small hands reaching for whatever was in front of her while I talked through projects and deadlines. A client scooped her up without asking, her gummy grin softening a conversation that had started stiff and formal.

"Your daughter is adorable," he laughed, bouncing her.

"She closes more deals than I do," I said.

He smiled, still holding her.

"Well, if she ever wants a job, tell her to call me."

Jodie pressed her cheek against his shoulder, content, unaware of the doors she was opening. She had her father's ease, I thought—Don's particular gift for making a room feel less formal simply by being in it. I watched her and felt something I had not always been able to feel without guilt: straightforward pride. Pride in my daughter. Pride in the life she was being raised inside. Pride in what I had managed, against considerable odds, to build around her.

Jodie's outgrown clothes caught on my hands, and I stopped.

I stacked her dresses into neat piles I couldn't bring myself to give away. Growing up poor in Ramallah, hand-me-downs weren't charity; they were survival. Maha wore dresses Yamma patched beneath the flicker of a single bulb, the needle flashing like a small blade fighting back scarcity.

"This will fit Maha—maybe you next year," Yamma

once said in Jerusalem, her voice gentle as she chose secondhand clothes, love disguised as thrift.

The wool carried the scent of Nablus soap and sun-dried laundry. Those clothes traveled through us—scraped knees, prayers stitched into hems. When they reached me, they already knew who we were.

I saw the same quiet magic in my own children. Adam's jeans cinched at Ramone's waist. Samuel, wearing shirts still shaped by his brothers' movements, the faint ghosts of their days lingering in the fabric.

Maha had worn Yamma's patches. My boys wore each other's shapes. The thread ran straight through. The same love, in different fabric, in a different country, in a different generation. We had carried it across the ocean without knowing we were carrying it. Now I was about to turn it into a store. That seemed right. That seemed exactly right.

The pile stopped growing. The idea fit.

All About Kids began to take shape in the quiet space I'd cleared. Families needed a place where good things could be used again. I wasn't just sorting fabric. I was piecing together the woman I had become.

Building inventory became a nighttime ritual. Tags snapped into place like quiet christenings. Each item carried a life once cherished.

One rainy Tuesday, a flyer slipped from the mail like an answer.

GOING OUT OF BUSINESS.

EVERYTHING MUST GO.

"This is it."

I did not sit with it. I did not make a list or call anyone or wait for a better day. I had spent enough of my life waiting for permission and better days and conditions that never arrived. I grabbed my keys. I drove through sheets of rain, wipers slashing time in half, the road blurring and clearing and blurring again. I was not calm. My hands were tight on the wheel and my heart was loud and I drove anyway, because I had learned—on a gravel shoulder in the dark, on a bathroom floor, at a bus stop with three boys and cold tokens—that you do not wait to stop being afraid. You move while you still are.

In the store, I didn't hesitate. I bought everything—blankets folded like clouds, onesies stitched with futures not yet lived, maternity dresses still holding the sweet Baby Magic scent of expectation. Box after box went into the van.

Adam and I turned Saturdays into expeditions. A thermos wedged between the seats, a folded map, a newspaper thick with red circles marking our route. I checked tags the way I checked produce—quietly, deliberately. I tested snaps, tugged at seams. Some pieces went back. Others stayed. I learned what lasted. Clothes built to outlast more than one childhood.

Yamma would have approved.

"Mom—look at this. Total steal." He grinned, arms full of baby clothes.

"Keep pile," I said, brushing dust from a tiny button.

"You always say that."

"And I'm always right."

At home, the living room surrendered. Boxes spilled

across the carpet. Fresh linen spray drifted through the air like a blessing. We scrubbed stroller scuffs with Murphy Oil Soap, its warm, familiar scent rising as we worked. We polished cribs until their wood caught the light, round and pale as new moons. Every item was tagged with care.

"Remember when we found this at the Johnsons' sale?" Adam asked, lifting a faded quilt.

"I'll never forget. That house smelled like cinnamon and chaos."

He turned a tiny shoe over in his hand.

"Mom, how does something so small carry so many stories?"

"The same way we do," I said. "One step at a time."

He looked at the shoe for a moment longer. Then he set it gently in the keep pile. I watched him do it—this boy who had been born eight months into violence, who had screamed stop hurting Mommy, who had placed his hand on my shoulder in a courthouse hallway and said it's okay, Mama, we're here. Handling a tiny shoe with care. Learning, without being taught, that small things carry weight.

Our home could no longer contain what we'd gathered.

Treasures crept into corners and closets. The storage unit became our second address, its metal doors clanging shut around a dream that was no longer imagined. The air held a faint bite of paint thinner from the shelves we'd built—evidence of work, intention, something growing too big to stay hidden.

When I began searching for a storefront, my prayers traveled with me, rising and falling with each mile. I drove slowly, scanning streets I'd never noticed before.

On a forgotten side street, I found it.

Faded brick. Ivy clawed at the mortar. Windows filmed with grime, dull and watchful like neglected eyes. The owner next door handed me the keys without hesitation. I unlocked the door and stepped in.

The air was thick, unmoving. Cobwebs clung to the walls, delicate and persistent, lace left behind by years of waiting. I stood there—beneath the dust, beneath the neglect—and felt what I had felt in the empty apartment in Germantown when the locks held and the boys slept through the night for the first time. Not arrival. Recognition. This place had been waiting. So had I. We were going to be useful to each other.

I invited Karen. Her tires crunched over gravel, the sound sharp in the quiet. She stepped out of the car and coughed as dust lifted around her.

"Halaina, you're crazy," she said, squinting at the building. "This place? It's a graveyard."

I smiled.

"I'm going to turn this place into something."

She crossed her arms, skeptical but curious.

"Show me."

I walked her through the space, careful not to rush. My voice stayed calm as dust stirred underfoot.

"Light will pour through these windows," I said, pointing. "Parents will browse. Children will laugh."

Karen let out a long sigh.

"If anyone can raise the dead, it's you."

She shook her head, laughing despite herself.

"When this place ends up gorgeous, I'm eating my words."

"Start warming them up," I said.

She groaned, rolling her eyes.

"I'm going to have to eat them, aren't I?"

I smiled, seeing it. And for a moment, standing there in the dust, even she looked like she believed me.

I reached an agreement with the landlord.

With Adam at my side, we dove in. Weekends dissolved into sweat and purpose, hours blurring together as we scrubbed, lifted, and scraped. Grime gave way inch by inch until sunlight broke through the windows, pouring in like something reclaimed, cobwebs vanishing as dust lifted with them.

I called my brother Frank in New Jersey, and he came down to lay and install the carpet he'd chosen. He built a platform for the glass display cabinet and the counter I had purchased from the going-out-of-business store. Frank, who had flown kites with me in the alleys of Harat al-Nasarah.

Frank, who had collected stamps and played marbles in circles drawn in the dust. Frank, who had grown into a man with calloused hands who came when I called. Some people in your life stay. I had not always known who those people would be. I knew now.

Above the door, I hung the bell myself. I had picked it out weeks earlier, turned it over in my hands in the store, listened to the way it rang—clean, bright, the kind of sound that says someone has arrived.

I stood on the step stool and fixed it into place and

climbed down and opened and closed the door twice, just to hear it. It sounded exactly right. I had built enough things by then to know when something was exactly right.

"Mom, it's really changing," Adam said one night, his face streaked, his eyes bright.

"It's becoming home," I told him.

And it was.

All About Kids took over the space. I made signs and set them into metal stands throughout the neighborhoods. I placed bold newspaper ads titled Treasures for Tomorrow's Adventures. Flyers curled on bulletin boards. Adam and I passed out business cards anywhere people paused—grocery lines, parks, waiting rooms.

A woman studied the card.

"I wish this existed when my first was born."

"It exists now," I said. "And I'm building it for moms like you."

Opening day arrived.

The bell above the door chimed as families filtered in, tentative at first, then smiling. A young mother bought a stroller and a bag of clothes soft as secrets, the clean scent of baby wipes rising as she shifted her toddler on her hip.

"I can't believe I found this here," she said.

"You'd be surprised what stories walk through these doors," I told her.

The register chimed—ka-ching—as my first dollar

slid across the counter.

I felt it.

The store blossomed. Parents lingered in the aisles, voices floating up as stories traded places. Behind the counter, a small TV played cartoons at low volume. Jodie sat in her high chair, cereal dust on her fingers, her spoon tapping the tray while I rang sales.

When her eyelids drooped, I laid her in one of the cribs waiting to be sold. A paper tag brushed her sleeve. I stood for a moment and looked at her—this girl born in a blizzard into a life that had finally, by then, become safe. Sleeping in a crib in a store I had built. Tagged gently, like something worth keeping.

On slow afternoons, she slid from her chair and joined other children near the shelves. Blocks knocked together. Toy cars traced the legs of dressers while their mothers sorted through racks and talked in half-sentences.

Jodie laughed easily, handing toys to children she'd just met, sitting close without hesitation. I watched from behind the counter as she learned belonging. She had not had to unlearn fear first, the way I had. She had simply started with belonging. I had given her that. I held that quietly, the way you hold something you are almost afraid to name in case naming it makes it fragile.

Sunlight warmed the edges of furniture, caught in the polish of cribs and bookcases, glowing along tabletops rubbed smooth by use. The store looked lived-in—not staged, not precious.

"Oh, that teether saved my sanity."

"I've been looking everywhere for a bouncer like

this!"

A tired mother laughed near the racks, bouncing her baby. Another nodded, relieved just to be understood. Children played in tucked-away corners, blocks clicking like soft music. The air carried the familiar scent of baby wipes. We hosted workshops, holiday gatherings, and arts-and-crafts sessions where glitter turned order into joyful chaos.

Then came the moment I'd whispered into that dusty air.

A Channel 7 News reporter stepped through the door, her gaze moving over the shelves, the families, the hum of life filling the shop.

"Is this new?"

I met her eyes. "Yeah."

She looked around. "You built all this?"

"I did."

"How?" she said, smiling.

"Late nights," I said. "And not quitting."

"You tell it beautifully. People will love this story."

"Can I do a piece for tonight?"

I nodded. "I'd love that."

She waved her cameraman in and flipped open her notebook, her eyes still roaming the aisles.

"How did you even know where to start?"

"I didn't," I said. "I just started anyway."

The segment aired that night. The boys crowded close, knees pressed to the couch, Jodie asleep in my lap. On the screen, the shop glowed—brighter than I remembered, fuller, alive.

"Mom's famous!" the boys shouted.

Adam squeezed my hand.

"Mom, you did it."

"No," I said, quieter. "We did."

Jodie stirred in my lap. The boys were loud around me. The shop was on television. I sat in the middle of all of it and thought of the kitchen table in Ramallah where Baba had read letters aloud and smoothed the creases before folding them again. I thought of Ibrahim in the basket on the bicycle, pedaling through streets I had memorized before I could speak.

I thought of Yamma's hands, folding and pressing and making do. I thought of all of it—and then I looked at my boys, and at my daughter asleep on my lap, and understood that this was what inheritance actually looks like. Not what is handed to you. What you build from what was taken, and what survived, and what you refused to let go.

The next morning, a grandmother came in holding a tiny dress.

Cedar clung to the fabric, the scent of careful keeping.

"I saw you on Channel 7 last night," she said.

"I didn't think anyone watched it," I said, smiling.

"Honey, you lit up that screen."

I handed a receipt to one customer and lifted a crying baby with the other arm. She went still against my shoulder, heavy and warm. The register chimed behind me. Laughter rose. Jodie's giggles drifted through the aisles. The bell above the door chimed loudly.

The once-dusty storefront filled with voices. Families moved through the aisles as if they belonged. The windows, finally clean, caught the sunset and laid it gently along cribs, tabletops, and glass. The glass reflected shelves, children, hands reaching.

The bell chimed again.

Another family stepped in.

I smiled.

The years the locusts had eaten—I was standing inside them now.

Rebuilt.

Not restored to what had been. Restored to something better. Something I had made myself, from what I had survived, for the people I loved most.

The dandelion does not mourn the wind that scatters it. It trusts the scattering. It sends its seeds into whatever ground will have them.

And then it blooms.

Chapter 14

BLOOM CROSSING

"Enlarge the place of your tent; do not hold back."
(Isaiah 54:2, NIV)

Our condo began to shrink as All About Kids grew.

Jodie—two and fearless—raced from room to room, toys scraping behind her. The boys—eleven, twelve, and thirteen—shared a single bedroom, sneakers piled at the door, homework spread across the floor, their lives pressing past the walls meant to hold them.

At night, I turned sideways through rooms that had once felt generous, stepping over backpacks and bodies.

It wasn't working anymore.

In the car, heat pressed against the windows as the AC hummed low. From the back seat, the boys' chorus rose again.

"Next one?"

It became our road-trip anthem.

Don turned onto a street lined with young trees and careful lawns. I watched the houses pass, leaning forward before the car slowed. Every For Sale sign pulled at me. At open houses, I counted bedrooms on my fingers, opened basement doors, stood in kitchens, imagined homework scattered across the island, voices calling out for help all at once. I was not looking for a house. I was looking for a life that finally had enough room in it. I had been in rooms that were too small for too long—by force, by circumstance, by other people's decisions about how much space I deserved. I was done with small rooms.

Weekends filled with open houses and long drives through neighborhoods that promised more.

This one did.

Bloom Crossing. Manassas Park.

Fresh asphalt gleamed under our tires. Saplings lined the curb as we parked. Sunlight stretched long across the model home floor, and for once, I didn't rush to fill the silence.

"Mom, look at this kitchen!"

Ramone's voice echoed as he disappeared down the hallway. I let him go. Let the sound travel. I had spent too many years in places where sound had to be kept small—voices lowered, footsteps careful, laughter calibrated. I stood in that model home and listened to my son's voice bounce off the walls and come back to me changed by the space, and I thought: yes. This.

Light slid across the hardwood as we stepped farther in. Our footsteps softened, absorbed. I paused in the doorway, listening—measuring how the rooms carried sound, how they might carry us.

Sun poured through the windows, clean and generous.

This would be our home—five bedrooms, three-and-a-half baths. A basement ready to hold work without pushing life aside. A family room wide enough for gathering. The kitchen island waited—homework spread wide. Upstairs, I could already see it—posters taped crooked, secrets whispered after lights-out, childhood dreams taking up space.

I did not need to think about it. My body had already decided.

Don hesitated.

"What if we get in over our heads?" he asked one night.

We sat at the kitchen table long after the house had gone still, papers spread between us like a map we didn't trust. I slid the school schedule toward him, then the sketch of the basement—measured lines, careful notes. Space for work. Space for living.

Don rubbed his forehead and stared at the numbers. The silence stretched. I waited. I had learned how to wait without filling the silence—how to let a person arrive at their own yes without being pushed. Finally, he nodded once.

After a few honest talks and a lot of prayer, we leaped.

The phone rang while I was folding laundry.

A sock slipped from my hands and landed at my feet.

I pressed the receiver to my ear and stood there as the boys shouted from the next room—life continuing without waiting for the answer.

When I hung up, my hands were shaking.

We listed the condo contingent on completion. A buyer came quickly—papers signed, dates circled. The closing landed exactly where we needed it.

At the table again, a check lay between us—crisp, real, undeniable. The check didn't just confirm the sale. It confirmed the risk. That we had leaped and the ground had risen to meet us.

Somewhere in it—in the timing, in the ease—I felt Maha.

Like a hand at my back, steady, letting me step forward. I had felt her before—in the doorway in Ramallah when she pulled me back from the ledge, in the hospital when I counted my own breathing, in the cockpit when I stood behind my boys and understood what I had come to give them. She had a way of arriving in the moments that required more courage than I had on my own. I did not question it. I only felt it, the way you feel a hand you cannot see, and you step forward anyway because the hand is there.

The moving truck pulled up, and the kids cheered.

"Call your room now or lose it!"

Adam bolted in, laughter ricocheting through the empty house. I followed them in. My footsteps echoed once, then disappeared under the thud of boxes hitting the driveway, voices rising. Laughter filled the rooms fast.

Each child claimed a room—blank walls, clean corners, space for posters and paint.

Adam took the basement bedroom with the private bath and painted the walls deep blue.

"It's my own apartment," he said, pride settling into his voice.

Ramone chose navy walls and taped his desk with hand-drawn superheroes, their edges curling as if ready to lift off.

Samuel painted his room hunter green, shelves filled with sports gear and trophies.

"Mom, check this out!" he shouted down the hall. "My trophies have their own shelf!"

Jodie's room caught the morning light. A hand-painted rainbow stretched across one wall.

"It's my rainbow house," she declared, spinning through a blur of red and yellow and blue.

I stood in the hallway between their rooms and listened to all of it at once—the pride in Adam's voice, Ramone's superheroes ready to lift off, Samuel's trophies on their own shelf, Jodie spinning inside her rainbow. Each one of them claiming space without asking permission. Each one of them completely certain they were allowed to be here. I had worked every year to give them that certainty. They did not know it yet. But they were living inside it.

Morning light filled the house.

Children rode bikes past chalk-covered pavement. From the neighbors, smoke curled from Big Ray's grill, drifting toward us like a welcome.

"You folks settling in alright?" he called out.

"Trying to. These kids act like they've lived here forever."

"That's the way it should be." He grinned.

Jodie thrived at the nearby private Christian school. Art found her early. Paint lived on her hands and sleeves, colors bleeding into one another without apology. Don and I traded morning drives, lingering at drop-off, taking in her chatter and the papers she brought home, speckled and proud.

The boys rode the bus straight from our driveway to Manassas Park High. Every morning, it pulled up like a quiet announcement. Doors folded open. They climbed aboard without looking back—independence, arriving on schedule.

Down the street, my sons folded easily into the Wran family. Amy had three boys close in age to mine—voices first, faces later, laughter doing the introductions.

"Your boys have good manners," she told me once.

"I can't take all the credit. Some of it is luck and prayer."

Big Ray ran an HVAC company. What started as pickup games spilled outward—ball bouncing, laughter carrying, teams reshuffling until the street itself felt claimed. Ramone and Samuel mapped mowing routes with the Wran boys, lawns divided and redrawn like small empires. They turned gigs into a system—clipboards, schedules, cash split cleanly. Soda sweated in their hands while arcade lights flickered. Evenings ended shooting hoops until dusk blurred the edges of the day.

Adam sat at the table with wires spread out before him, soldering iron humming low. He barely looked up.

"I'm going to build something big."

"I know you will."

He paused, checking his work.

"You already are."

After being expelled at sixteen, Adam went to work for Big Ray. I did not pretend it was not a hard thing. It was. I had watched him bend over wires and notebooks and prototypes since he was old enough to hold a soldering iron, and the expulsion felt like a door closing. What Adam showed me—slowly, without announcement—was that doors closing are not always what they appear to be. He went to work. The days were long and physical. And still, at night, the notebooks filled with speaker designs. He sent rough prototypes overseas and waited.

"They're actually writing me back," he said one night.

"Of course they are. You did the work."

Ramone moved differently—deliberate.

"I'm finishing, Mom," he said once.

And he did.

Graduation day arrived. A cap flew. Of all my boys, he was the one who crossed that stage. I watched him walk and thought of the incubator. Two pounds. Just keep breathing, habibi. He had kept breathing. He had done more than that. He had walked across a stage in a cap and gown and I had sat in the audience and understood that this was the distance we had traveled—from a machine breathing for him to a diploma in his hands. I did not try to contain what I felt. I let it be as large as it was.

In my eyes, he had never been anything less.

Samuel never stopped tinkering.

"Mom, look what I made!"

Parts scavenged, repurposed, brought to life—his creativity moving faster than language.

Time with Big Ray's family deepened what we learned at home—skills hardened by work, steadied by example. Evenings hummed with music and homework chatter, the oven breathing out the scent of eggplant, tomatoes, and warm spices. Pots clinked. Pages turned. A song played low enough to let voices stay first.

Sundays smelled like qatayif—sweet cheese pancakes—folded and browned, the aroma drifting through the hallway like a remembered season. Yamma's kitchen in the hallway of a house in Virginia. The thread still holding.

Jodie's laughter floated down the stairs, a ribbon of sound threading through this new life.

The doorframe filled with pencil marks. They climbed steadily upward, names and dates stacked as the kids stretched taller. I had started the marks when we moved in—just a pencil and a wall and a child standing straight. By the time the marks reached the top of the frame, the children would be grown. I knew that. I marked them anyway. Evidence. We were here, and we were growing, and there was a wall that knew our names.

Some afternoons, I sat on the porch while bikes rattled past and laughter moved down the block.

Diane's question came back the way certain songs do. Not when I invited it. When the house quieted enough for it to find me, it threaded through dinner, through the clink of forks and the scrape of plates. It hovered at the sink while hot water ran over my hands, steam fogging the window. After bedtime, when the rooms finally exhaled, it lingered beside me like a presence that refused to be dismissed.

By then, the question had worn a groove in me.

"Have you ever thought about becoming a hairstylist?"

At first, I dismissed it.

But after five years of working seven days a week at All About Kids, I made the decision.

I sold off the remaining merchandise. The closeout stretched over two months. Racks thinned. Shelves emptied. Each sale felt like a small goodbye.

When the SOLD sign went up, nostalgia washed in—the shop stood quiet, shelves bare, children's laughter still in the walls. I walked All About Kids one last time. I ran my hand along the counter, past the bell above the door that I had hung myself, through the space where Jodie had slept in a crib with a paper tag brushing her sleeve and where mothers had stood in the aisles relieved just to be understood.

"It was a good run," I whispered.

More than that. It was proof that I could see something where others saw a graveyard and make it bloom. I would carry that knowledge into whatever came next.

I gave myself a few months to stay home on

purpose—to be present with my children, to reset, to listen for God in the quiet. Mornings slowed. Afternoons softened. Still, the invitation tugged.

One day, on a whim, I stopped by the academy.

The door opened to a hum of motion—the snip of scissors, the hiss of spray, voices weaving in and out like choreography. Mirrors caught fragments of faces, hands in motion, hair falling in clean lines to the floor.

A student looked up.

"First time?"

"Yeah. Just looking."

She nodded. "I'll get Diane for you."

She said it like she'd been expecting me.

I lingered at the counter, fingers resting on the edge of an enrollment form. Doubt pressed in, familiar and insistent. I knew this feeling. I had felt it at the hotel in Tysons Corner, hand on the door handle. I had felt it at the bus stop with three tokens and nowhere to go. Doubt was not new. What was new was that I no longer let it finish my sentences.

Then Diane's voice rose over it.

"You'll be amazing. You're a natural."

The noise around me faded. The room narrowed to the page, the pen waiting. I thought of Mrs. Smith: you're doing so well, Hala, keep practicing. Nancy firming my handshake. Mike sliding the paper across the counter. The woman at the bench pressing an address into my palm with warm fingers. All of them saying, in their different ways: there is something in you worth developing. I had been given that gift more times than I had counted. I was not going to refuse it again.

Yes.

This is my path.

The pen dragged across the page.

Late nights and early mornings followed.

I practiced wherever I could—between classes, after school, in borrowed hours. Neighborhood kids lined up in folding chairs, feet swinging, trusting me with their heads.

"Don't make me bald, Miss Halaina!"

"I wouldn't dare. Your mama would never forgive me."

Hair fell in uneven lines at first. I learned to breathe through it. To slow my hands. Jim, a local barber, watched quietly, then stepped closer.

"Steady now. I've got you. All good barbers had a first shaky cut."

Those hours settled deep. Muscle memory formed. Confidence followed.

At Potomac Hair Academy, under Diane's leadership, I pushed myself further than I thought I could. When I graduated with honors, my instructors pulled me aside.

"You'd be great. We'd love you to teach."

"I'm honored. I belong behind the chair."

I worked in various salons—budget-friendly chains and high-end establishments—each offering lessons, though not always pleasant ones. In some, professionalism slipped. In others, everything looked polished but respect was thin and clients moved through chairs like numbers. I noticed. It began shaping something else—an insistence on warmth, real connection. I started taking names, quietly telling my clients I was opening a salon.

For the next two years, I drifted—clocks on the wall, mirrors too clean, time pressing in.

I learned what didn't fit. I stopped saying yes to anything that tried to hurry me. In the space that opened, a new image began to form.

A chair. A mirror. A place built for listening.

I could feel it waiting.

At home, a different kind of work began. With the contractor's help, we carved the basement into a studio. Soft-pink walls rose where concrete had been. Sleek cabinetry settled into place. A vintage sewing-machine base became my styling station, sturdy and sure.

Life had taught me that the best foundations are the ones that have already held something else. Steadiness is not born—it is earned through use.

Donna called, introducing herself as a sales rep for Cosmoprof. She asked if she could stop by. When she arrived, we talked among unopened boxes and bare shelves. She took in the space, then said it simply.

"I'll front your first order. Pay it back in six months. No interest."

"Are you sure?"

"I know a rising stylist when I see one."

She was another one of them—the people who

arrived without being summoned and offered something before being asked. I had stopped being surprised by them. I had started being ready. Boxes followed me home. Bottles clicked into rows. Brushes found their places. Empty shelves filled with intention.

The morning of the unveiling came quietly.

I wiped the chair once more. Adjusted the mirror. Smoothed my apron.

Enter as strangers, leave as friends.

Come in with a handshake, leave with a hug.

Mrs. Johnson arrived at ten.

"You ready, sweetheart?" she asked.

"As ready as I'll ever be."

Halaina's Salon found its rhythm quickly.

I paid Donna back before the six months were up. A check slid across the counter, early and exact.

I had learned that lesson young—from Yamma counting coins before they left the house, from Baba smoothing creases in letters before reading them aloud. You honor what people give you. You pay it back. You pay it forward.

Loyalty returned as clients brought stories with them—laughter, heartache, hope.

The scissors found their cadence. The chair learned to listen. A handshake when they arrived, a hug when they left—the rhythm holding, chair by chair.

For years, I had lived braced for impact.

Here I was, shaping a sanctuary with my own two hands.

As my work bloomed, serious problems at home began to surface.

Don moved through the house without looking up. Conversations shortened. Silences stretched longer than necessary.

I recognized the particular quality of a silence that is not peaceful. I had lived inside enough of them to know the difference between a quiet that rests and a quiet that waits. This one was waiting. My shoulders were tightening again—not the old tightening, not fear of what a man's hands might do. Something different. The tightening of a woman who has built something real and feels it beginning to shift beneath her.

That night, I locked up the salon. The air still held the day—hairspray, warmth, voices lingering where bodies had been. I turned the sign. I felt the shift.

Change.

My hand reached for the switch. The room went quiet.

Outside, the street was the same as always. But inside me, something had shifted—some plate beneath the surface grinding slowly against another. I had rebuilt before. I had rebuilt from nothing: broken windows, three bus tokens, a wired jaw. I could rebuild again.

The question was what, exactly, was about to need rebuilding.

Chapter 15

PRUNED TO RISE

"Better is a dry morsel with quiet than a house full of feasting with strife."
(Proverbs 17:1, NIV)

Dryers roared. Scissors shhhk-ed through hair. Voices moved between the chairs. Foils crinkled.

Then the sound thinned, pulling away—as if I were hearing it through glass instead of standing in the room I had built.

I stopped mid-cut.

I had felt glass before. The church in Bethesda, where I stood in white and my body was there, but I wasn't. The courthouse hallway where I smiled without opening my jaw. That glass had been put there by someone else—by force, by fear, by conditions I had not chosen.

This was different. This glass had formed slowly, from the inside, until even the salon around me felt far away. I was standing there with scissors raised, and I was behind the glass.

That was the moment I understood it clearly.

By then, the silence had been building for years.

Shears rested in my hand, my phone in the other. On

the screen, Don and I smiled—close, polished, the kind of photo people trust. The longer I looked, the more it felt practiced. Two people arranging themselves correctly—two people who had learned each other's angles and forgotten each other's faces.

In the dark edge of the screen, my reflection stared back—composed, capable, and out of place in my own life.

I had spent years learning to read rooms. The particular stillness before something breaks. The way a house sounds when the people in it are managing instead of living. I had learned those sounds in Ramallah, in basements, in places where close attention was the thing that kept me safe. I did not want to be paying that kind of attention in my own home. But the body knows before the mind admits it. Mine had been paying attention for a long time.

At home, we were already drifting—not fighting, not breaking, separating without noise.

He had become someone I didn't fully recognize. Not transformed—just gradually turned away, the way a room gradually turns dark when no one notices the light changing.

We stopped meeting. He leaned toward Jodie, and I leaned toward holding everything together. At three years old, she already knew how to pull him.

"Princess decides," he'd say, smiling.

And he meant it.

At first I told myself it was love—a father besotted

with his daughter, which was not a terrible thing to be. But there is a difference between adoring a child and letting a child carry the weight of your emotional life. Jodie was three. She was not meant to be anyone's anchor. And slowly, without announcement, that is what she was becoming.

One night, I asked,

"Do you want to go to dinner?"

"Let's ask Jodie," he said.

I stood there. Something in me snapped—not loudly, the way things used to snap in that marriage before this one. Quietly. The way a thread gives when it has been pulled past its limit for the last time.

Bedtime shifted, rules softened, decisions bent around her. And where Jodie was indulged, the boys were corrected. Where she was heard, they were dismissed. It wasn't loud. It was constant. And constant is worse than loud, because constant doesn't give you a moment to recover. It just keeps going, day after day, until the shape of normal has changed and no one can remember what it looked like before.

Children know. They always know.

One evening, Samuel stood in the doorway, his shoulders tight.

"It's not fair."

I stepped toward him.

He pulled away.

I stood there after he left and held what had just happened. Samuel, who at five years old had reached for my chin with sticky fingers and asked is Baba a bad man. Samuel, who had sat beside his brothers in a courthouse hallway with his legs swinging, waiting for me. Samuel, who had pressed close in the dark and said we love you Mama. He was pulling away from me now—not because of anything I had done, but because of what he was seeing, what he was learning to carry alone. A child should not have to manage alone. I had not managed to protect him from that, and I felt the weight of it settle into me and stay.

Adam stopped trying as hard. Samuel withdrew. The house didn't explode—it shifted. Family nights changed, laughter thinned. Jodie's voice filled the room while the boys made themselves smaller.

I had worked every year to make sure they never had to make themselves smaller. And here it was happening again, in the same house, at the same table, and I was watching it and could not stop it alone.

I tried to talk to Don—more than once.

"This isn't balanced," I told him. "They feel it."

He didn't see it, or didn't want to.

Every conversation ended the same.

"Whatever."

"They're fine."

They weren't. Neither were we.

Each evening, I stepped upstairs from the basement salon, hoping he would look up. Most nights, he didn't.

"Hey," he said, eyes still somewhere else.

Not connection. Just acknowledgment. A placeholder where a person used to be.

I thought about the first night. The hotel in Tysons

Corner. His hand resting on the cushion between us, palm open, waiting. I wasn't used to that, I had thought then—being given room. I had held that open palm for years like a promise. Now his eyes were somewhere else every evening, and I was the one doing the waiting, and the room between us had grown into something I did not know how to cross.

One night, I brought it to the surface.

I slid a list of counselors across the kitchen island.

"Don... we need help. Please."

He didn't touch it.

The paper lay on the island between us, and he did not touch it, and I understood in that moment—the way you understand things that have been true for a long time and that you have been refusing to look at directly—that the list of counselors was not going to fix what was broken, because the broken thing was not a problem he was willing to name. You cannot repair something with someone who will not admit it needs repairing.

"I don't need a stranger in our marriage," he said.

Something in me shifted—final, quiet. Not dramatic. Not the kind of shift that announces itself. The kind that simply completes, the way a door completes its closing—no slam, just the soft click of a latch finding its place.

By the time he agreed, it was too late. I had already stepped back inside myself. I didn't have the energy to keep holding it together. I had held things together through a war zone, a basement, a fryer, a wired jaw, a bus stop, a stripped kitchen. I was not a woman who gave up easily. I had learned the difference between endurance and hope. Endurance keeps going because it has to. Hope keeps going because it believes something will change. I had run out of the second one.

I went to counseling alone.

The counselor listened, then said one word.

"Separate."

I sat with it.

It didn't shock me. It confirmed something I had been carrying without permission to set down. The word arrived and the weight I had been holding shifted—not lifted, shifted—the way the not-going shifted at Dulles when I finally walked through the departure door. Still heavy. But moving in the right direction now.

It confirmed it.

We stayed under one roof for the kids. He moved downstairs, and I stayed upstairs. We became two lives sharing a structure—not partners, not enemies, just in between.

We coexisted carefully.

He still showed up in quiet ways—helping with homework, fixing things, stepping in when needed. There was no doubt Don loved the boys and me.

But we didn't feel it.

I have thought about that distinction many times since. Love that is present but not felt. Love that exists in a person's chest but does not travel across the room. It is not the same as no love. It is its own particular ache—knowing the feeling is there and being unable to receive it. I do not blame Don for what he could not give. I only know what the house felt like, and what the boys felt like inside it, and what I felt like stepping upstairs each evening into a silence that had stopped being peaceful.

I was not the woman I had been in the hotel parking lot, forehead against the steering wheel, shaking before she walked through the door. I was not the woman on the bench with the cold tokens. I was not the woman on the floor of the bathroom in the shelter, pressing her wrist to the sink.

I was still standing.

I had built a salon in my basement and a store on a forgotten side street and a life that my children were growing up inside of, tall and loud and certain they belonged.

Whatever came next, I knew how to begin it.

I had begun before.

Chapter 16

NEW LEAVES

"Forget the former things; see, I am doing a new thing!"
(Isaiah 43:18–19, NIV)

The very first night I slept alone, I left the hallway light on. Not out of fear. Out of habit.

That distinction mattered more than I could explain at the time. For years, lights left on had meant something else—the particular vigilance of a woman who slept with one part of her mind always listening. This was different. This was just a habit that hadn't yet caught up with the fact that I was safe. That is what peace feels like at first, when you have not had it for a long time: it feels like habit you haven't broken yet. The body takes longer than the mind to believe it.

The bulb cast a thin line beneath the bedroom door. I watched it from the bed, waiting for footsteps that didn't come.

Morning came without interruption.

I rose before the alarm and stood barefoot in the kitchen, palms flat against the cool counter. The house did not press against me or lean. I stood there. I drank my coffee at the window instead of the table. Outside, a sprinkler ticked across a neighbor's lawn. Water caught the sun and broke into light.

Something in me loosened. Not relief—more like space opening. The particular expansion of a room when the furniture that was too large for it has finally been moved out.

I walked back to the bedroom and opened the closet.

I began with the hangers.

At night, I scrolled through listings in the dim hallway light, the phone warming my palm. My chest stayed tight.

The next day, I told a realtor,

"I'm just browsing."

She glanced at me over the rim of her glasses.

"Just browsing is how most big changes start."

A few days later, an old friend called. His mother had died. He spoke slowly, weighing each sentence before letting it go.

"She had a two-bedroom condo," he said. "Warm light. A screened-in porch. Trees outside every window."

Coffee cooled between us. He slid a set of keys across the table. They landed with a decisive sound. I have thought about that sound many times since—the particular finality of a key set on a table by someone who has decided to give something away. It is not the same sound as anything else. It means: this is yours now, if you want it.

I hesitated.

"Are you sure?"

He nodded once.

"She'd want someone like you there."

I drove straight to Niki Place, palms damp on the steering wheel.

When I opened the door, light spilled across the floor in a wash of mosaic color.

"Oh my God," I whispered.

I walked slowly, my fingertips brushing the walls. The rooms held their quiet without asking anything of me. That was what I noticed—the absence of demand. I had lived, for most of my life, in spaces that required something from me the moment I entered them. Vigilance. Performance. Smallness. These rooms simply held their quiet and waited.

I could see it—Jodie curled into the couch, the porch washed in afternoon sun, the air moving gently through open screens.

Not relief—something steadier. Recognition. The way you recognize a place you have never been but somehow already know. As if some part of you had been holding a picture of it, all along, without knowing what you were holding.

The price stayed. The process moved easily—papers aligning, signatures landing clean.

As I signed the final document, something settled over me. Steady. The way Maha used to calm me without saying a word. Not a voice. Not an image—just a steadying certainty, the kind that settles without asking to be understood.

The pen lifted. The ink dried.

For three months, I remodeled in secret.

Most evenings, when Don thought I was with friends, I drove to the condo instead. I unlocked the door, stepped into the quiet, and got to work.

I swept up what the contractors left behind, hauled out dust and splintered scraps, and painted room by room. Sawdust clung to my hair. Grit settled into my arms. My shoulders ached—the honest kind of ache that comes from changing something with your own hands.

There is something particular about building in secret. No one is watching, which means no one can approve or disapprove. There is only the work and the room and the slow transformation happening between them. I had built things before with people watching—the store, the first salon, the storefront Karen called a graveyard. This was different. This was just me and a paintbrush and a future I hadn't told anyone about yet. It belonged entirely to me in those hours. I was the only one who knew what it was becoming.

The place shifted under my hands. The kitchen began to catch light. The bathroom softened into a retreat, the sunken tub waiting. The laundry nook found its rhythm.

Every nail. Every stroke mattered.

By mid-summer 2003, the furniture was in place. Boxes emptied. The rooms breathed.

I had decided.

That evening at Outback Steakhouse, the scent of blooming onions hung thick in the air. Plates clinked.

Laughter drifted from nearby booths.

Don stirred his coffee longer than necessary, the spoon tapping faintly against the ceramic—his tell when he didn't know what to say.

I folded my napkin once, then again, my fingers trembling.

"Don," I said softly.

He looked up.

"I'm leaving."

I couldn't stay and keep losing myself.

The words settled between us—sharp, precise. His eyes widened, then narrowed, as if rereading a sentence he didn't understand.

"You're serious?"

"I am."

A pause. The hum of the restaurant filled it.

"Do you already have a place?"

"I do."

I told him the truth—that the late nights I said I was with friends had been spent somewhere else. Preparing. Painting. Carrying pieces of a future I hadn't yet named out loud.

He stared into his coffee, the surface trembling slightly as he set the mug down.

"Didn't see that coming," he said.

"I tried," I whispered.

"I know."

Two words. He said them without defense, without argument. Just acknowledgment. I had expected more—more resistance, more confusion, more of the conversations that ended in whatever and they're fine.

Instead, he said I know, and the simplicity of it undid me a little. It meant he had known something was coming. It meant part of him had been watching it arrive and had not known how to stop it. That was its own kind of grief, and I held it alongside mine.

We talked logistics. Quietly. Carefully. Like two people packing up a shared room without touching the same box. Jodie would stay with him—for stability, for routine. I would remain woven into her days, unchanged in all the ways that mattered.

I kept my life folded away, unwilling to let my unraveling spill into a space meant to hold others.

Around us, plates landed. Orders were called out. A server topped off a water glass. The restaurant continued, indifferent, as it always does when the large things happen quietly at small tables.

Even after the separation—after the divorce—I kept working out of Don's home, my scissors still cutting, my hands steady.

I was still gone. But Jodie didn't need to feel it all at once. Children can absorb change if it comes in pieces, if the people around them stay recognizable. I was still her mother every morning. Still the person who knew which cereal she wanted and how she liked her hair. The address had changed. Nothing else had to.

My clients never knew—no announcements, no explanations, no cracks showing. I kept my voice even, my hands sure, my smile intact. I didn't want to unsettle anyone, didn't want my private fracture to ripple through a space built for comfort.

For two more years, I worked from the same chair and mirror. The rhythm held. Routine steadied Jodie. Every morning, I unlocked the door, turned on the lights, and stepped back into the life I knew how to manage—cutting, listening, holding—while the rest of me waited, quietly, for the next leaf to open.

After the news broke, I took Jodie to see the condo—her room waited empty and bright.

"Mama, this is our castle!" she said, spinning from doorway to doorway, arms wide.

"Then let's make it shine," I told her.

It was late afternoon, a week after I moved in. Light settled through the windows as hummingbirds hovered just beyond the glass, their wings a quiet blur, as if they had come to witness something I had finally claimed for myself. I stood at the window and watched them and thought of the bench at the bus stop, the tokens cold in my palm. I thought of the empty apartment in Germantown, the boys' voices echoing off bare walls. I thought of every space I had entered with nothing and made into something. This was another one. The last one, I hoped. The one I had earned most clearly, because I had chosen it with the clearest eyes I had ever had.

Inside, the condo carried the scent of home—kifta sizzling in the pan, harissa warming nearby, spices lifting from the kitchen like memory made visible.

My place held the quiet, the effort, the beginning—no longer borrowed, no longer shared, mine.

The divorce itself surprised me with its gentleness.

Pens scratched paper. Pages slid back and forth. At one point, we laughed—small, unguarded—a brief recognition of the years that had been good. There had been good years. I did not want to forget that. Don had given me room when I didn't know what room felt like. He had stood beside me at the sink washing dishes and beside Samuel on the homework and beside all of us at the shelter in Fairfax with aprons tied too loose. Those years were real. The ending did not erase them.

Don pushed the papers toward me and paused.

"Fair's fair," he said, handing me my share.

"Thank you," I whispered.

With the proceeds, I rented out the condo and bought a home in Bloom Crossing—the same subdivision where Don and Jodie lived. Familiar streets. Familiar trees. Fresh-cut grass and new blossoms lined the sidewalks, the air carrying that unmistakable scent of beginnings.

The walkout basement stood unfinished—concrete floors, open studs, light spilling in where walls would someday rise. Raw, unclaimed—waiting. I recognized it immediately. I had always been good at seeing what a space could become.

I met with a contractor in the bare basement, our voices bouncing off concrete.

"I want it clean," I said. "Black and white. Modern."

He smiled, already measuring the room with his eyes.

"That'll cost more."

"Then I'll work more," I said.

And I did.

Walls went up. Lines sharpened. The basement shed its rough edges and became a salon—sleek and deliberate. Glossy counters caught the light and gave it back, softened. From the bathroom, a faint citrus scent drifted through, clean and quiet. From the sitting area, you could see everything.

The dryer station settled with a gentle tap-tap. The washing station answered with a deeper, hollow knock. The front desk drawer closed with a precise click. Each sound marked its place. Each corner found its rhythm.

A television murmured in the corner—morning news, weather, the low comfort of houses being redone somewhere else. Sometimes I switched it to XM. Christian music slid into the room. Beyond the glass, the deck opened to the golf course—wide green stretching out, softening the edges of the space, letting breath move freely.

In the kitchenette, coffee stayed hot. Cold drinks waited in the fridge. Nothing extravagant. A room built to listen.

About a month before opening, I began quietly telling my clients—one by one. Just around the corner. Nothing else had to change.

"Are you okay with that?" I asked.

The answer was always the same.

"Yes."

Their ease steadied me. I printed flyers. Ran a small ad. Let word of mouth do what it always does when trust is already in place.

At a Chamber of Commerce meeting, I found myself standing in a hallway between sessions when a man stepped forward and offered his hand.

His name tag was clipped neatly to his shirt.

"George," he said. "I'm with Chick-fil-A."

"I've heard you're opening a salon."

"I am," I said. "Just down the street."

He smiled—warm, unhurried.

"Let me sponsor your grand opening."

For a second, the hallway noise fell away.

"Sorry?"

"I'd like to sponsor it," he repeated. "Consider it a blessing for your new beginning."

I laughed, caught off guard. He was another one of them—the ones who arrived without being summoned, who offered something before being asked. The woman at the bench. Joe Reiber saying yes. Donna fronting the first order. Now George from Chick-fil-A in a hallway. I had stopped questioning why they came. I had started simply saying thank you and meaning it.

"Then you have to be there," I said. "For the ribbon cutting."

"Of course," he said. "I wouldn't miss it."

I stood there a moment after he walked away, my hand still warm from the shake.

The grand opening glowed. Warm light caught on champagne flutes. Chick-fil-A trays lined the counters. Familiar faces filled the room, voices rising and folding into one another. I moved through it slowly, shaking hands, smiling, breathing it in.

Mrs. Johnson rested her hand on the countertop.

"It's beautiful," she whispered.

Mr. Davis from the Chamber nodded once, looking around.

"This place," he said. "It's going to be a hub."

Jodie tugged at my sleeve.

"Mama," she said, eyes wide. "You did it."

I brushed a piece of confetti from her hair.

"No, baby," I said. "We did."

After that, momentum carried me.

I bought a second condo, gutted it, rebuilt it with my own hands, and rented it out. The checks arrived on time—predictable—proof of a life I had learned how to build and maintain. I still craved stability—benefits, something solid beneath my feet—so I earned my CDL.

"You're a natural," the trainer laughed as I eased the bus through a tight turn, hands steady on the wheel.

Each morning, Jodie climbed aboard, hair still sleep-soft.

"Bye, Mama."

"Have a good day, honey."

I drove the route and thought about Baba driving the wrong way down a one-way street, the horns blaring, both of us laughing until we couldn't breathe. I thought about the bicycle, the basket, the wind on my face before I was old enough to know where we were going. I had always been carried by people who knew how to move. Now I was the one driving. That felt right. That felt like something he would have smiled at.

The edges with Don softened. Hand-offs became simple. A nod. A pause. An unspoken agreement held between us. Whatever broke, we had protected her. One evening, porch-swing shadows stretched long across my Bloom Crossing home as I held Jodie close.

A soft breeze moved through the yard, lifting the edges of the quiet. She rested her head against my shoulder, legs tucked beside mine.

"We're okay, Mama," she murmured.

I kissed the crown of her head.

"Yes," I said. "We are."

The house behind us settled, and in that pause—between the swing's slow arc and her slow breath—I felt it: the turn already made, the next chapter opening without announcement, waiting for me to step forward. I did not rush toward it. I sat with my daughter in the evening light and let the pause be what it was—complete. A moment that did not need anything added to it. Those are rare. I had learned to recognize them.

The salon stopped being just a business.

It became the place I stood upright again—feet planted. I poured myself into the work—into listening, into shaping, into helping women recognize themselves again in the mirror. I knew what it was to look into a mirror and not recognize the person looking back. I knew what it was to look into one and finally see yourself clearly. That was what I was offering, chair by chair. Not just a cut. A moment of being seen.

I took on more. Said yes to what I once would have

stepped around.

Evening settled in. Lights stayed on. Chairs filled.

I stood behind the mirror and did the work—steady, present, finally my own.

I had been so many things in so many rooms: a hidden girl, a translated voice, a woman running through glass, a mother counting breath in the dark. I had been all of those things fully and completely, and none of them had broken me, and this—this woman standing behind a chair in a room she had built, in a life she had chosen—was what they had been making, all along.

I did not need to say it out loud.

The room already knew.

Chapter 17

ONE TREE, THREE BRANCHES

"I am the vine; you are the branches."
(John 15:5, NIV)

I carried my three boys—Adam, Ramone, and Samuel—the way I carried groceries up narrow apartment steps and laundry down basement stairs: one trip at a time, arms burning, jaw set, praying nothing would slip.

That prayer lived everywhere I did.

In the car, it became a whisper, hands tight on the wheel while traffic stalled. Over a sink full of dishes, it turned into something mouthed, steam rising, the boys arguing down the hall, voices colliding.

My children grew anyway—not neatly, not evenly, but outward. Three directions. The same root held.

ADAM – The Builder

Adam came out gripping—like a fighter—and dreaming like a builder.

He was born in July 1984 at Holy Cross Hospital in Silver Spring, Maryland. Outside, heat pressed hard against the windows, summer heavy and unmoving. His small body lay beneath the soft blue wash of phototherapy lights, skin tinted gold with jaundice. I slipped my finger into his palm. He closed his hand around it—firm. His eyes stayed open, tracking the light as it moved across the room—measuring, alert.

I held him close, breathing him in, hope and worry rising together. I didn't know what paths he would carve or how many times he would rebuild. He was here. That was enough.

As a baby, he was easy in a way that made me think he didn't need much.

There's a photo of him gripping a dollar bill before he could walk—fingers tight, knuckles pale, eyes serious as if he understood the weight of holding on. He slept when the room went quiet. Watched more than he cried. I'd cross the room, fold laundry, turn back—and realize he'd been there the whole time, still and observant.

Toys didn't stay whole long. He pulled them apart with careful hands, studying how pieces fit, where they resisted, where they gave way. Legos and wooden blocks spread across the floor. He sat cross-legged in the middle, shoulders hunched, head bent, building something only he could see. The house moved around him—dishes clinking, a door closing, a television murmuring—but he stayed fixed.

"Adam, it's bedtime."

"One more part, Mom."

A pause. A click. Something shifted into place.

"I think I figured out how to make it spin."

His face tightened with focus—someone solving something that mattered. I stood there watching the pieces turn beneath his fingers, disappearing into the work.

Between building on the floor and growing taller than the kitchen counter, Adam loosened his grip. Not all at once. Enough. We'd be walking, and his hand would slip from mine without asking. He stayed close—not attached. I'd reach out. Then stop. His hand loosened—and mine let go.

The days found rhythm again. Lunches packed. Alarms buzzing. Backpacks thumping onto the floor. One morning, Adam walked ahead and didn't look back. I slowed without meaning to, my hand half-raised. He kept going. It stung first. Then it steadied.

His curiosity hardened into focus at ten. He spent hours assembling model cars and airplanes, tiny parts spread like a private language. His hands were small but sure—testing, correcting, starting over. When the computer entered our house, he moved toward it immediately. While his brothers played, Adam built.

He called me over.

"Mom, look what I made it do."

Green code filled the screen, lines blinking into place.

"You're teaching yourself what people pay to learn."

"Guess I've got your stubborn streak."

Nights blurred as we set up the shop—hangers clicking, new clothes whispering as boxes opened. We worked until 2 a.m., side by side, sleeves rolled, tape clinging to our fingers.

"Maybe even franchise," he said.

When he was fourteen, I took him to meet Dave, the

owner of Milwaukee Custard.

"Firm handshake," I said. "Eye contact."

He nodded. Dave smiled.

"That's a solid handshake, young man."

A beat.

"You're hired."

The next day, Adam stood behind the counter, air thick with chocolate and vanilla. He came home smelling of sugar.

"I'm scooping ice cream now," he said. "Watch me."

Ramone looked him up and down.

"Congrats. You finally found a job where eating half the inventory is part of the training."

Adam grabbed a napkin and snapped it at him.

"Jealousy doesn't look good on you."

"Nah—I just don't trust a guy who smells like dessert all day."

Their laughter moved down the hallway—loose, familiar. I watched from the doorway, unseen.

His ambition outgrew the job before the uniform wore thin.

"Mom—this is fun. But it's not enough. I've got bigger plans."

Later, the house went quiet. The basement didn't. Marker scratching. Tape ripping. Bass moving through the floorboards. He adjusted. Listened. Started again.

"These speakers don't just play music," he said. "They're mine."

"Why speakers?" I asked.

"Because everybody listens to music. I want to build what they hear."

Night after night, he chased a sound he couldn't hold—adjusting, listening, starting again. Then one evening, he looked up.

"Mom… I contacted a supplier in China."

I remember the pause that followed, the weight of it. They could build what he designed. Weeks later, the boxes arrived—fifty speakers—sold out. Then more orders came.

"They're here," he said. "Listen."

The bass rolled through the walls.

This wasn't noise.

It was his.

Then school turned hostile.

Meetings that went nowhere. Tension that built in hallways and conference rooms that smelled of bad coffee and worse intentions. Don—the administrator—had decided what Adam was before Adam had finished becoming it.

"You think you know everything," Don said.

Adam's jaw tightened. His hands stilled. When he finally spoke, his voice was low and even.

"At least I'm building something with my life."

Then came the word: expulsion. Hard. Final.

"I won't let this define me," Adam said. "Watch me."

Later—

"Mom, school's not for me. I need to focus on my business."

"You're only fifteen."

"You didn't wait for anyone to save you."

He left with a jacket in his hand, shoulders squared like he'd made the decision long before that moment. The apartment with Nicholas was cramped, roach-infested, the air sour.

"Mom, this place isn't great. But it's temporary. I've got ramen, a dream, and a notebook full of plans. I'll be fine."

After the call, I didn't move. The room stayed too quiet.

From that apartment, he got his GED—quietly, finishing what he started. Then he got to work, learning by touch—parts, engines, frames—building something out of whatever he had.

"Mom, I sold another one today!"

The bikes came next.

"Why motorcycles?"

"Speed and sound go together. If I can build what they hear, I'll never be broke."

By seventeen, he signed a lease.

"My place. My business. My life."

"You did this yourself," I said.

"So did you."

Then everything accelerated. Contracts came faster. Inventory turned over constantly. Long flights to China. He found scale with Costco, moving overstock at volume, real numbers finally taking shape.

For a while, it worked. Then it didn't. Margins tightened. What once moved easily started to stall.

He didn't sit in it. He pivoted.

E-Yard Recycling Solutions became his next move—an online junkyard built from high-end cars that couldn't be salvaged. He tore them down, cleaned each part, and sold them piece by piece. What started as survival turned into something larger—an appliance store, a roofing company, work that stretched in every direction. Even where he lived, he stepped in—leading the HOA, solving problems the same way he always had: hands-on.

"I've got big plans for my new home, Mom."

"You always did."

"Roots first," he said.

He nodded.

"Then wings."

By forty, he was a single father raising two teens. His days stretched wide—work, calls, movement without pause.

"Mom... this is bigger than anything I've done."

His eyes still held that same light—the one I first saw tracking the phototherapy lamp across a hospital ceiling, measuring, alert, already reaching for something just outside his grasp.

Some nights, when everything settles, I whisper it to no one in particular.

You did it, Adam.

You built it.

RAMONE — The Fighter

If Adam had been born a builder, Ramone was born a fighter.

He was pushed into the world early.

Born at Holy Cross Hospital in Maryland. Two and a half pounds, skin translucent, barely bigger than my hand. They wheeled him immediately—the NICU—an incubator sealed shut. Warm light pooled over him, a mechanical hum filling the room as tubes and blinking numbers tracked every breath.

I stood on the other side of the glass, hands empty. I wanted to hold him. I couldn't.

Terror and guilt arrived together and didn't separate for days.

The NICU was heat and tubes and numbers that decided everything—measured drops of milk, seconds between breaths. A body learning how to swallow, how to stay warm. Every ounce mattered. A stalled day pulled me back to the edge. I leaned toward the incubator and whispered,

"Keep growing, baby... I'm right here."

I told myself he would live. I said it until it began to sound true. His fragile body worked constantly—swallowing, adjusting, taking drops at a time. Five pounds. That was the number they were waiting for.

The light stayed with me. The hum. The way he fought to stay. The day I brought him home, his spirit arrived before the quiet ever could.

Frailty didn't soften him. Colic didn't dull him. The cries were sharp and relentless, dragging the nights beyond endurance. With Adam only nine months older, the house felt like twins without balance. The cycle never stopped. Nursing them both at once left my arms aching, my head spinning. Ramone cut through the haze. The scent of baby powder lingered in the air. His skin was silky. I held him close and whispered through tears,

"You're home with Adam."

The difference between them was unmistakable. Adam watched—quiet, observing. Ramone claimed the room. Pick me up. Don't you dare forget I'm here. I never did. What formed between us wasn't gentle—it was unbreakable.

By eight, his intuition startled me. If I entered a room carrying worry, he knew. He climbed my shoulders without a word, small hands kneading the knots there, serious, focused. He never asked what was wrong. He understood. He stayed until the tightness left.

As he grew, his gifts appeared early. The teachers kept circling back to the same line:

"He learns fast—already ahead of the class."

That quickness stayed with him—a sharp mind paired with mischief, the kind that drew other kids close instead of pushing them away.

Adam opened a brand-new box, tape still stiff at the seams. Ramone got a yard-sale find, wrapped in yesterday's newspaper. Once, I brought home a small alarm and handed it to him.

"You can attach it to your bike."

He turned it over slowly, studying it like an experiment. Then he pressed the button.

BEEP.

He looked up at me, completely serious.

"Perfect, Mom. If someone steals my bike, I'll chase them into returning it."

He clicked it again.

BEEP.

"See? Crime solved."

He laughed and drifted away. Sarcasm became his armor—landing the joke before anyone else could.

At home, he folded himself into the lives of his younger siblings—Jodie and Samuel. Their joy ran loud and unfiltered, ricocheting through the hallway—the sound that told me my children were still children, safe for that day.

In the afternoons, he and Samuel hunched over the Monopoly board, money everywhere, rules loosened just enough to suit him.

"You're cheating!" Samuel protested.

Ramone grinned, eyes sharp.

"Then catch me."

Another bill slid under the table.

When Jodie was born, Ramone was eleven—old enough to understand the weight of being a big brother, young enough to feel the wonder of it. He adored her immediately. If she fussed, he rocked her with a seriousness that stilled the room. If she cried, he rested a careful hand on her back, humming nonsense until her breathing slowed.

He became the quiet center between them—pulling a laugh out of Adam, comforting Jodie when her feelings spilled over. His sarcasm stayed tucked away until it was safe to surface. As the years passed, the bond drew tighter. Jodie trusted him without thinking—a thread between them that never frayed.

Once, she came home with tears streaking her cheeks, schoolyard cruelty still clinging to her. Ramone sat beside her on the porch swing. The wood creaked under their small weight.

"Tell me what happened."

She wiped her face, voice shaking.

"They said I was weird. They said nobody likes me."

Ramone shook his head. Not angry. Certain.

"Well, they don't know you. But I do. And I like you more than anybody."

Her smile came slowly, lit by his words.

At fourteen, he joined Adam at Milwaukee Custard, determined to earn his own money. Scoops clattered. Cones piled high. Sugar hung heavy in the air. Wiping sticky hands on his apron, he smirked at a customer,

"I'm not saying I'm addicted to ice cream, but I'm willing to go to rehab for it."

Beneath the sparkle, I caught something quieter—a need to be seen without the joke doing the work.

"You joke your way through everything," I said once.

He shrugged.

"Laughter's cheaper than therapy, Mom."

When he landed at Jay's Heating and Air, something settled—the heavy tools in his hands, the rhythm of real work, men who showed up, taught him, counted on him. It grounded him. When Jay retired, he followed Adam back to Maryland, into salvage-yard heat and noise. Metal clanged. Voices overlapped. Laughter spilled out of the garage and into the driveway.

It worked. Then the split showed.

One night, Ramone sat heavy with it, jaw tight.

"I can't do right in his eyes."

I kept my voice low.

"You both carry the same fire."

He nodded once.

"That's the problem."

"And the blessing."

He looked at me.

"We're too alike, huh?"

"Maybe," I said. "Brothers like you—you're branches of the same tree. You just reach in different directions."

At thirty, he moved to South Carolina looking for a reset. Living under the same roof reshaped our days—shared meals, late-night talks, laughter moving through rooms that once held strain. Thread by thread, we stitched closer.

Ramone loved to tease.

"Mom, you held me six months, then pop—like a champagne cork."

He laughed, bright and loud, but his eyes dimmed just enough to reveal him. That was him—blunt, magnetic. Living together wasn't simple. Love didn't erase it. We were rebuilding something we had lost. His drinking crept in, loud and disruptive, bringing disorder with it.

He was working at Air Doctor Heating & Air Conditioning. The work fit him. Problem-solving. Long days. Service calls demanding patience and focus. He showed up before the doors unlocked. Stayed after the trucks were parked. Listened more than he spoke. His boss noticed.

He stayed late to double-check the wiring. He left houses better than he found them.

One day, a regular client sat in my chair and mentioned her air conditioner had gone out. She described the technician who came—how he stopped to admire her herb garden before getting to work.

"I sent him home with a bundle of herbs," she laughed.

Something in her voice stopped me.

"What was his name?"

"Ramone."

I looked at her.

"That's my son."

She smiled.

"He was a very nice young man. My husband and I really liked his work ethic."

I held that compliment like proof of his character.

We fought—hard. Words flew unchecked, sharp enough to wound. One night, his voice tore down the hallway, loud enough to rattle the frames on the wall. My phone was already in my hand, thumb hovering over 9-1-1, my heart pounding so hard the screen blurred.

"Mom... don't," he choked, suddenly small.

His shoulders dropped. The fight drained out of him as fast as it had ignited.

He called me names that cut deep. I fired back. I'm not proud of either of us in those moments. What I remember most is standing in my own hallway feeling like a stranger in it—wondering how love and this could exist in the same house at the same time.

More than once, I stood there with the phone in my hand, threatening the police. He didn't leave. And every time, when the dust settled, when regret clouded his eyes, he would sit on the edge of my bed or pause in the kitchen doorway, his voice barely holding together.

"Mom, I don't mean it."

I sat beside him, legs shaking. It came in uneven steps. He tried harder than anyone I'd ever known.

That's when he adopted Tinky.

That little dog helped him when I couldn't. Tinky curled tight against his side.

He reached for a beer. Then stopped.

His hand hovered there longer than necessary.

Later, he tried to explain what those moments felt like.

"Another day. Another struggle."

Cooking helped. He moved through the kitchen with quiet purpose—chopping, stirring, tasting. Garlic sizzled in oil. Steam clouded the windows. The sports channel murmured in the background. His hands stayed busy. His mind steadied. The edge in him eased.

"I'm no chef," he grinned, stirring the pot. "I can burn a meal with love."

Not every night held that peace. Some nights, the drinking won. Arguments split open again—sharp, volatile, familiar. After one more fight, something settled in me. I couldn't keep living like that.

"Ramone," I said quietly. "I love you. But we can't keep doing this. You need space. And I need peace."

He packed slowly. In silence. No yelling. No theatrics. Within a week, he found a one-bedroom apartment—small, worn, barely furnished, but his. A place where he could breathe. Where I could breathe. Where love could stretch without breaking.

The first time I visited, the rooms echoed with emptiness—mismatched plates, a sagging couch, a bed pushed against the far wall. There was stillness there, too.

"This is it, Mom," he said softly. "My place."

Renee had two children—a daughter and a son with autism—and Ramone opened his heart to them without hesitation. He stepped into their lives, learning their rhythms and the unspoken rules of their days.

Ramone wanted children of his own. He carried it quietly—in the way he lingered near families in public, in the softness that came over his face when he held someone else's baby. When it didn't happen, he carried it the same way. He calls Tinky his daughter.

He loved them, but he was never fully allowed to stand in the space of a father. Decisions were made around him, not with him. He stayed anyway. Learned the schedules. Showed up when it was inconvenient. Cooked. Fixed what broke. Tried again when things unraveled. That was how he loved.

He taught her son small victories—brushing teeth, tying shoes, using the bathroom—celebrating each one with a soft pride that lit his face.

Once, I asked him why he stayed.

He looked down. His voice dropped.

"Because he needs me, Mom. Somebody has to show him what staying looks like."

Over time, the fighting grew louder than the love. In the end, Ramone chose peace and walked away.
Now it's just him and Tinky. A small place. A quieter life. What had once frayed between us found its way back—laughter and late-night conversations. At forty, he lives quietly. The past still follows, but it no longer leads.

"Ramone, you're my hero," Jodie tells him. "I don't have to say it. I see it."

He never wanted me chasing after him. He never asked for affection. I learned what he needed instead—shared meals, unspoken pauses, choosing to stay when leaving would've been easier. Some children need their names called. Ramone didn't. He needed presence.

And I was. Still am.

He fought to stay from the very beginning.

He still does.

SAMUEL — The Endurer

He arrived late summer, 1986. Plainfield, New Jersey. Heat pressed against the windows. Cicadas droned their tired chorus.

The house was still carrying the weight of Nicholas's violence. Years of it had carved tremors into my bones that I couldn't always feel until I was still.

Samuel arrived in the middle of that chaos—early, small, fragile. This time, there was no incubator waiting. When the nurse placed him in my arms, everything stilled. Six pounds, five ounces—solid, present, real. His skin was velvet. His head smooth beneath my hand, that new-baby scent rising warm and clean.

He quieted me.

"You made it," I whispered, my voice breaking. "You're safe now, baby."

He was an easy baby. The kind whose laughter carried through the house and reached places grief had hollowed out.

Ramone adored him from the start. They grew up shoulder to shoulder—two boys barely a year apart—racing bikes until dusk, battling over Monopoly, inventing their own summer mischief. Their laughter moved through the house, filling rooms that had known too much silence.

The years with Nicholas—the bruised nights, the words I learned to swallow—had taken that version of me from Adam and Ramone. Fear had made me careful. Tight. Always listening. Samuel got the mother who could finally breathe—the one who knelt, who laughed without flinching.

Centreville Elementary had its own smell—cafeteria bleach biting the air, warm paper trays stacked too high, melted cheese clinging to everything. We'd landed in a new routine—new streets, new schools, the boys finding their place again. That's where their bond got loud.

One day, I joined them for lunch. Pizza steamed on plastic trays. Overcooked vegetables slumped in their corners. The room buzzed—voices rising, chairs scraping, milk cartons popping open. My boys never shrank from me. Never pretended I wasn't theirs. When they saw me, both heads snapped up.

"Hey guys—this is my mom!" Samuel called out,

grinning. "Don't mess with her."

A beat.

"She's overprotective."

He let it sit just long enough.

"Like... licensed."

Laughter rippled across the table. Samuel soaked it in. I ruffled his hair, felt the heat of him under my palm, the certainty.

As he grew, his temper came fast—sharp, then gone. A slam. A shout. Then quiet. Underneath it was a heart that never learned to guard. He gave without measuring—his money, his food, his time—whatever he had, whenever someone needed it.

A soft place. My heart outside my body.

When he was fourteen, he started his first real job at Milwaukee Custard, working alongside Ramone and earning his own money. The smell of waffle cones and melting ice cream clung to their clothes. Scoops slapped metal bins. Customers laughed. The boys joked back, easy and loud, as they moved behind the counter.

"If this doesn't work out," Samuel said once, sliding a cone across the counter, "I'll open my own place and hire myself."

He imagined new flavors, dreamed up promotions, invented ways to fix what didn't work.

That same year, his curiosity took over our garage. One summer afternoon, grease and oil stained his hands as he crouched over a battered scooter. A lawnmower engine had been strapped on crooked. Wires snaked everywhere. The rest was held together with duct tape and confidence.

"It's ready, Mom!" he yelled, eyes bright. "Mostly."

I had no business climbing onto that thing. I did it anyway. I tore down the street, wind in my hair, the engine rattling beneath me. For a breath, I was fourteen again—free, careless.

The scooter bucked. The pavement rushed up.

I hit hard.

Pain shot through my foot. My arms scraped raw. My face burned. Samuel laughed—until I didn't get up. His face emptied.

"Oh my God, Mom," he said, voice breaking. "I'm so sorry."

Later, with my foot broken and propped up, we told the story and laughed until we couldn't stop. The scooter became legend—his wild creativity, my foolish bravery, our lives stitched together in the most Samuel way possible.

By seventeen, classrooms couldn't hold him. Engines could. Money in his pocket. Steel and grease in his hands.

"School and I agreed to see other people."

He never graduated. He walked away.

He found his way to Japan Star, where used Honda engines were imported and rebuilt. Tools clanged through the space. Oil and metal clung to the air and his clothes. He learned systems. Solved problems. Earned trust.

"You're running this place with me now," the owner

told him. "You've got a head for this."

He took it seriously. He came to know every corner of the shop—kept orders straight, made sense of the chaos. He stayed nearly a decade.

When the Manassas store closed, the owner asked him to relocate to Albany to help keep the store there afloat. I drove up with him for the move. He showed me the city—brick row buildings, tired storefronts, streets older than their repairs.

We went to a small downtown theater, the kind with faded carpet and seats installed before knees were invented. Our legs jammed forward. Neither of us could settle. Samuel leaned over and murmured,

"I think this place was built when people were shorter and complained less."

We made it through most of the movie out of stubbornness, then went to dinner, stretching our legs as we'd earned it. The next morning, I flew home, leaving him in the chapter he was trying to build.

Albany wore on him. The shortcuts. The decisions that made no sense. It scraped against his pride, against his belief that if you were going to do something, you should do it right. He came back to Virginia not long after.

"Turns out," he said dryly, "I'm allergic to bad management."

Later, on the phone one night, I could hear him leaning against the counter, grease still streaked across his hands.

"Maybe it's time I do my own thing," he said.

I pictured him already halfway there—engines

humming, plans lining up.

"You've got the drive," I told him. "Just make sure you build it on solid ground."

He laughed.

"You always worry too much, Mom."

"Someone has to," I said.

He didn't argue.

He left Japan Star and joined Adam in Maryland, stepping into the salvage-vehicle business. For a while, the scrapyard felt like their shared kingdom—clanging metal, stripped-down cars, parts scrubbed clean and listed online. Engines torn open. Doors stacked like ribs. Fire met fire.

"I can't work like this," Samuel said one night, staring at the floor. "I mean—I can. I don't want to."

The strain of that season showed. He talked less. Slept light. Restlessness crept in.

"I don't need a boss," he said, half-smiling. "I need a steering wheel."

He built a moving company from grit and stubborn hope. He drove the U-Hauls himself. Lives in his hands. The business grew fast—homes, couches, boxes marked FRAGILE.

"Relax," he'd tell them, lifting a box like it weighed nothing. "I've got this."

Years later, visiting Jodie in Virginia, I texted him—not sure he'd answer. He did. We met for dinner and sat across from each other, years of distance stretched tight between us, loosening as the plates emptied and the words came easier.

"I've been living out of my car, Mom."

A beat.

"I'm working," he added, almost defiant. "It's temporary."

He laid out his plans and asked me to be his partner. I listened, weighing the years against the man in front of me—tired, determined. I didn't become a partner. I believed in him. I mailed him the check.

"If you ever want a fresh start," I said, "my place in Myrtle Beach is open."

He nodded once.

"Good to know."

Then, softer:

"Thanks, Mom."

The phone rang not long after.

"I'm ready for a new beginning, Mom."

Boxes of merchandise stacked in the corners. Nissan Skylines lined the driveway—proof of how hard he'd been working. Marley tore through the house after my dog Chico, nails skittering across the floor. The days filled fast—work, laughter, his business taking shape.

At night, we slowed down. We cooked together—mostly him. I chopped when he let me. He handled the heat, the seasoning, moving through the kitchen like it was second nature. Afterward, we watched movies—bowls of popcorn between us, butter slicking our fingers. Horror was always our pick. Whenever someone split from the group, he'd mutter,

"Safety in numbers."

I'd flinch at the jump scares. He'd laugh, halfway through the popcorn.

"If anything grabs you," he said, eyes still on the screen, "I'll fight it."

I snorted.

"You didn't even look."

"Didn't need to," he said. "Safety in numbers."

Before he headed out to meet clients, I'd stop him at the door.

"Never walk into a client empty-handed."

He'd pause, keys in hand.

"Even if it's donuts," I added.

He sighed, long-suffering.

"Especially if it's donuts. And a firm handshake."

"I know, Mom," he said, turning back toward the car.

He'd come back with a pink box tucked under his arm, confidence settled on his shoulders like the meeting was already his.

"People trust a man who brings sugar," he said once. "It means he planned ahead."

Space tightened. HOA notices piled. Rules pressed in. Walls thinned. Old patterns crept back—pride, stubbornness, fear—quiet at first, then louder. We circled carefully, trying to hold the good while something underneath strained.

I was buying a single-family home. Before I moved in, I hired my cousin to install the vinyl flooring. He drove down from New Jersey confident he could handle it. I paid him. I stayed out of his way. Or tried to.

I cleaned as he worked—scraps lifted, edges swept, dust chased into corners.

"Why is this such a mess?" he snapped, pointing at the floor.

I looked down. The scraps were his.

"I cleaned," I said quietly.

He waved me off. Later, he shoved the cutter into my hands.

"Go ahead. Cut this."

I did.

"No," he said immediately.

It wasn't a discussion. It was noise. He yelled. He screamed. The house was empty, the sound bouncing hard off bare walls. Stepping back was worse. The tension grew heavy—pressure stacking day after day.

Then I felt a pop in my head. Sharp. Sudden. The room tilted.

The stress had settled into my body—dizziness, exhaustion, a fog I couldn't shake.

A hospital bed replaced my kitchen chair. A stroke kept me there seven days.

Overhead, a loudspeaker crackled.

"Dr. Jackson, report to the ER."

The door swung open. Samuel stepped in, carrying a food container. He leaned close, set it on the tray, and whispered,

"Hope you're hungry."

He pulled up a chair, and we talked—errands, traffic, plans for the next day. Ordinary things. The kindness of ordinary things.

After long nights alone with my thoughts, I knew what I had to do. I asked him to move out. The words broke something in me even as they left my mouth. He didn't argue. He didn't posture. He found a place near Ramone, a few houses away. The distance stretched—quiet, unfamiliar, heavier than miles.

A window unit he no longer wanted. A return to Lowe's. A gift card I meant to hand back. Between my intention and his understanding, something twisted. I heard the knock before I saw him—that particular knock that means something has already gone wrong.

He showed up at my home, shoulders locked, eyes sharp, and accused me of stealing the unit. Right there, in front of my clients.

"You took my air conditioner," he said, voice raised.

My client froze mid-sentence, her hands folding into her lap as the room tipped.

"Sam..." I said, my throat closing. "That isn't what happened."

He turned away, breath hard, jaw clenched, leaving my salon thick with words that never should have been spoken.

The police. Two officers at my door.

And the video on Facebook.

I watched it once. Only once. My own stunned face flickered back at me from the screen.

"God, Sam... why?" I whispered into the room.

The room didn't answer. In the days that followed, hurt and confusion knotted. How could he do that? So publicly? Even through the ache, something held. Not forgiveness. Not yet. Understanding.

Two years passed before I reached again toward the light—this time with my hands busy. I poured myself into digital albums for my children—new software, new hardware, programs I had never touched. I scanned hundreds of photos, restored faded faces, pulled color back into years gone dull. I spent more than I should have on the frames, but it was Christmas. I wanted each of them to feel seen.

Every album became a prayer.

Where we started. What we survived.

When I mailed them out, Adam called. Ramone called. Jodie called. Gratitude moved easily between us. Samuel refused his.

"Take that back to her," he told Ramone.

Then the text came. Sharp. Deliberate. Aimed straight at my faith, my worth. I read it once. Then again. The pain opened, slow and hot.

"Keep your gifts. Keep your faith."

The words landed like stones I didn't have the strength to lift.

Love didn't disappear. I sent one last message.

"I love you too. Merry Christmas."

My hand shook over every key.

I ran into him in passing—at gas stations, at red lights. Each time, he turned away.

I didn't chase. I didn't harden.

I didn't close the door.

Hope stayed.

Beneath the noise, beneath the anger, beneath the distance, I still believe the boy I raised is there—the one who loved loud and bright.

Some bonds aren't solved in the moment.

They're carried.

A cord of three strands is not quickly broken.

Chapter 18

STEMS UNBROKEN

"Whoever is kind to the poor lends to the Lord."
(Proverbs 19:17, NIV)

Sunlight slid across Jodie's bookshelf, catching the edges of her open books.

"Mom, do you want to hear this?"

The crooked bun loosened at the nape of her neck, the highlighter bleeding through the page, her lips moving as she traced each line. The desk lamp cast a small, stubborn circle of light, leaving the rest of the room in shadow. Pages rustled as she turned them, careful not to lose her place. A pencil rested behind her ear, forgotten. Her shoulders leaned forward, intent.

The little girl who once devoured picture books on the living room floor had grown sure. She didn't look up. She didn't need to. I stayed where I was, unseen.

I had known, from very early, that she would be like this. Not the books specifically—the sureness. The quality of her attention. The way she moved through the world as if it had been arranged for her to understand it, and she intended to. I had prayed for that when she was still inside me. I had sung it into her before she had ears to hear it.

While I was pregnant with Jodie, I used to sing to her in those quiet moments.

The apartment would fall still, and my voice filled the space between us. I'd sit on the edge of the bed, one hand on my stomach, letting the melodies spill out—half lullaby, half prayer. Those songs were our first thread. I did not know then what she would become. I knew that I was talking to someone—that there was a person arriving, and I wanted her to know, before she had words or a face or a name, that she was coming into a life where someone was already watching for her. Already glad she was coming.

"Do you hear me, sweet girl? It's just you and me."

The blizzard of '96 raged outside, smothering Fairfax Hospital in Virginia under a thick layer of snow.

"Please, just get me there," I whispered to Don. "I can't wait much longer."

My contractions came hard and close together. The lights flickered. The halls hummed. Outside, the storm pressed against the windows while the building ran on emergency power. Everything felt suspended—as if the world had narrowed to breath, pain, and the moment about to break open.

At six pounds, Jodie burst into the world—her first sharp cry cutting through the storm's howl, my raging storm baby. She had been fighting to arrive since before the blizzard. The storm did not slow her. That was the first thing she told me about herself.

Her warmth gathered against me, her steady rhythm pulling the room into a strange, holy stillness.

I had fought for her—through bed rest, IV drips, and the constant shadow of fear. This moment was ours.

Her fingers curled around my thumb as if she knew me. Protectiveness rose through me.

She's a fighter, I thought, her wide eyes taking in the room, awake to everything. I had thought the same thing about Ramone, standing on the other side of the incubator glass. But Ramone had been fragile first and fierce second. Jodie arrived fierce. She had not needed to earn it.

The colic came like a storm of its own—relentless cries echoing through the house. Nights blurred into one long stretch of pacing as I walked the same worn path, bouncing her on my shoulder, whispering lullabies, promising it would pass—until Ms. Frances, our neighbor with soft hands and a gentler voice, stepped in.

She'd scoop Jodie into her arms and sway with that slow, sure rhythm only grandmothers and angels seem to know.

"Give her here, sweetheart."

Her humming softened the air, and Jodie's cries melted into hiccups, then sleep.

By the following winter, we took a trip to Florida in search of warmth—but panic found us instead. Her breath hitched. Her nose clogged, thick green mucus sealing each breath. She strained beneath my hand, working too hard for air. Heat radiated from her skin.

The room closed in. I counted—each breath, each pause—waiting for the next to come.

"It's okay, Jodie. Mommy's here."

She healed slowly—a gift we didn't take for granted.

By two, her brilliance was already breaking through. I stood at the counter, spelling the word stupid to myself. Without looking up, she said,

"Mom, that means 'stupid.'"

Her mind soaked up anything that resembled learning—phonics tapes, bright workbooks, even the shapes-and-sounds software I had downloaded when I built ARS Publications.

One evening at dinner, she dipped her tiny finger into the Tabasco bottle before I could stop her—curious, fearless. She touched it to her tongue, blinked hard, then broke into a grin.

"Hot!"

"More?"

That was Jodie entirely. Not cautioned by the first burn. Already asking for another.

Reading became our nightly ritual. Goodnight Moon was her treasure.

"Mommy, can you read it the silly way? Again, Mommy!"

I read it every way she asked. There were nights I was exhausted beyond reason, and I read it anyway, because she was asking, and she would not always ask, and I knew that, and I was not going to waste the asking.

Jodie begged for a toy I couldn't afford. When I said no, she dissolved into tears that wouldn't stop.

I warned her I would spank her if she didn't calm

down. And when she didn't, I followed through.

"Mommy, I'm sorry," she sobbed.

"Are you going to stop crying?" I asked.

"Yes, Mommy..." she managed between shaky breaths.

To this day, she giggles when I bring it up. That is Jodie's grace—she does not hold the imperfect moments against me. She turns them into stories we tell together, laughing at both of us.

Turning ten widened her curiosity, and it softened me.

She got her first period that year—on my birthday. Unlike Yamma, I sat her down and explained everything gently. I thought of the folded paper towel pressed into my palm on a sidewalk in New Jersey. I thought of the nurse who said congratulations and the words that moved too fast for me to catch. I was not going to give Jodie a paper towel. I was going to give her understanding.

"Mom... do you get your period like me?"

I nodded, grateful to guide her through what I had once faced alone. That is the thing about surviving something without help—you become determined that no one you love will have to.

Don and I had split, and she lived with him full-time. I still saw her. Months slipped by without her under my roof. I moved back to Bloom Crossing to be closer. Visits were awkward, cues often missed, and late-night talks followed.

"Mom... will I see you tomorrow?" she whispered.

The question landed every time. Will I see you

tomorrow. I had asked versions of that question my whole life—of Maha, of Ibrahim, of everyone who left. Now my daughter was asking it of me. I made sure the answer was always yes.

As she grew into those in-between years—old enough to read alone, still young enough to slip her hand into mine—bookstores became our sanctuary.

We moved slowly through the aisles, the smell of coffee and paper in the air. Warm cups in our palms, she drifted from shelf to shelf, pulling down one book, then another, as if each spine were a doorway she might step through.

At fifteen, she left Virginia and moved to Myrtle Beach to be with me.

We were rebuilding what Rick had fractured years earlier—his sharp words and cold dismissals chipping at her confidence long before she understood why someone meant to protect her chose to hurt instead. There were days she came home, shoulders pulled in, and whispered:

"Mom… why is he so mean to me? I didn't even do anything."

I heard that question and felt something ancient and familiar move through me. I had asked versions of it in basements and hotels and courtrooms. Children should not have to ask it. I ended my relationship with Rick and bought a small townhome near Socastee High School. She slept through the night.

She stayed late for mock trial. Papers spread across the kitchen table long after dinner plates were cleared.

Mock trial became her stage.

She stood when it was her turn, shoulders squared, notes untouched. Her voice didn't waver as she cross-examined the witness, each question measured and deliberate. The room quieted. Even the adults leaned in. She took control of the space—calm, prepared, unafraid—and settled into herself.

Not bravado—authority.

I watched from the back of the room and thought of the girl on the school stage in New Jersey, moving her mouth without sound, waiting for her family's faces in the rows and not finding them. This was what the other side of that looked like. My daughter, in a room full of people, unafraid to be heard.

On weekends, she practiced archery until her fingers reddened. If there was a sign-up sheet, her name was on it. In archery, she set her feet, lifted the bow, and drew the string back to her cheek. She didn't rush. She breathed, released, and watched the arrow cut cleanly through the air before landing dead center.

No celebration—just a quiet nod.

She already knew she'd hit it. She was confirming, not discovering.

After graduating from Socastee, she went to Mary Baldwin College and threw herself into theater.

Rehearsals stretched late. Scripts followed her from room to room, margins crowded with notes.

She spoke about characters the way other people talked about friends, as if they lived just beneath her skin.

"Mom, I want to pursue acting. I think... this is where

I'm meant to be."

She traveled to London—alone, brave, determined. She surfaced from the Underground into cool rain—heavy air, traffic surging around her. Big Ben tolled above the street, its sound cutting cleanly through the movement below. Red buses hissed past. Tires whispered against wet pavement. The stone beneath her shoes was slick with rain. She adjusted her coat and stepped into the current of strangers.

When she crossed the Thames, the wind tugged at her sleeves. She slowed midway, hands on the railing. The river slid beneath her—brown, restless, carrying everything forward. She stood there longer than she needed to.

From the heart of Piccadilly, she called me, buses groaning, voices overlapping in the background. When she spoke, her voice carried the city with it—footsteps, a faint echo of bells.

"Mom, I'm walking everywhere," she said.

"I know," I answered, picturing her in motion.

She ducked into bookshops like Waterstones Piccadilly, where the noise fell away—paper, dust, old wood—and staircases rose without signs telling her where to go. She sat on the floor beside a shelf, back against the wall, reading without urgency, without looking at the clock. No one rushed her. No one watched. She moved through the city the way I never could at her age—unafraid, unclaimed, belonging only to herself.

"I don't want to leave," she said later, softer.

I didn't tell her what it cost me to hear that. The cost was nothing to regret—it was pride, the particular kind that aches because it is so complete. She had gone somewhere I had never been, alone, and she had not wanted to leave. That meant she had arrived somewhere fully. That meant she was free in a way I had wanted her to be free since before she had a name. I let it be enough that she could say it. I let her have it.

In 2023, I walked those streets.

I crossed the bridge where she had stopped, felt the wind press against my coat, and heard the bells carry across the river. The city moved just as she described—steady, indifferent, alive in its own rhythm. I followed her path, stepping into corners she had already made her own. I found familiar spices tucked into side streets—Middle Eastern kitchens breathing warmth into the cold air, a quiet reminder of home in a place that wasn't mine.

I learned the rhythm of the Tube—descending into its tunnels, reading the lines, moving with the current instead of against it. What once would have overwhelmed me became simple: follow the signs, trust the path, step where others step.

In a bookshop, I stood where she had once sat and let the quiet settle. Shelves rose around me, the scent of paper and wood thick in the air. For a moment, time folded. I could almost see her there—legs tucked beneath her, lost in a page, unhurried, unafraid.

I wasn't following her anymore.

I was meeting her there.

That is what children give you, if you let them—new places to stand. New ways of being in a world you thought you already knew. I had carried her through a blizzard and a fever and a colic night and a bad relationship and a mall meltdown and a question whispered in the dark: will I see you tomorrow. She had carried me into a London bookshop and shown me how to sit still without apologizing for it.

We had been carrying each other all along.

After leaving Mary Baldwin, she worked at a daycare, then moved into nannying to support her education.

Mornings started early—backpacks by the door, small shoes lined up by the mat.

"Jodie, can you tie my shoe?"

She learned the rhythms of other families' homes, the quiet responsibility of being trusted with what mattered most. Parents spoke to her the way people talk to family—confident, grateful, at ease.

"We don't worry when you're here. She listens to you."

Seeing how she was with those children—the way she knelt, listened, offered comfort—I knew she would be a patient, kind mother. She had that in her from the beginning. The way she rocked her doll with seriousness. The way she handed toys to children she had just met in the store, sitting close without hesitation. Belonging was something she had always known how to offer.

Her compassion deepened with age. One weekend in Virginia, we stopped at a light where a woman stood near the median, her coat too thin, her hands buried in her sleeves.

Jodie didn't hesitate—she unbuckled her seatbelt, reached into the back seat for the snacks she always kept with her, and leaned out the window.

"Here you go. I brought extra today."

The woman's face softened—surprise, then relief. The light changed, cars pressed forward, and a hush settled over us.

I had carried that truth for years—the baker who said for Um Ibrahim, never; the neighbor who handed me what she could on the first night; the woman at the bench with warm fingers pressing an address into my palm. Kindness given without calculation, without waiting to be asked. There it was, living in my daughter, in a car, at a red light, as naturally as breathing.

She had not learned it from a lesson. She had absorbed it from the life she was raised inside.

At twenty-seven, she came for a visit.

What had been buried broke loose.

It came fast, without warning. Her voice rose, sharp and raw, filling the room. Words tumbled out, tangled with years I hadn't known how to reach. She paced the space between us, hands clenched, movement jagged. Rage rolled out of her in waves—physical and impossible to miss.

I stood there stunned. A truth surfaced that had lived inside her for years. I had never seen her like this. The house seemed to shrink around us as what had been swallowed finally demanded to be heard.

Then she paused, inhaled, and said:

"You hear me... but you don't listen."

She wasn't asking for comfort. She was asking to be met.

"I need you to listen to me, Mom. Really listen."

I stood in that room and let it land. All of it. I did not defend myself. I did not explain. I had spent years telling my story, finding words for what had happened to me, learning how to be heard. My daughter was asking me to give her the same thing. The least I could do was stop talking and receive her.

We both cried.

I apologized.

Not the quick apology that closes a conversation—the kind that costs something, that sits with the weight of what it is acknowledging. I had not always been present in the ways she needed. The separation had left gaps. The years of rebuilding myself had sometimes left less of me available to her. She had carried that. She deserved to say so. And I deserved to hear it without flinching.

Slowly, we rebuilt a bond shaped by respect rather than assumption. Sometimes she asked for advice only to dismiss it. Sometimes silence felt safer. Sometimes listening was all I could offer. I learned to offer it without attaching conditions to it—without needing her to receive it a particular way, without needing her to confirm that I had done enough.

She began to trust me with the full version of herself. That is the thing you work toward with a daughter. Not the easy version. The full one.

As my children stepped into their own lives, a different kind of quiet moved in.

For the first time in years, there was space.

And in that space, I began to meet myself again.

Not the girl who had hidden behind Yamma's dress. Not the woman who had learned to disappear. Not the mother counting breaths in the dark. Myself—the one who had been there underneath all of it, waiting with more patience than I had ever given her credit for.

She had things to say.

I was finally ready to listen.

Chapter 19

SHEARED, SAVED BY GRACE

"Do not take revenge, my dear friends, but leave room for God's wrath, for it is written: 'It is mine to avenge; I will repay,' says the Lord."
(Romans 12:19, NIV)

My children were growing. My faith held. In Bloom Crossing, the salon thrived—scissors clicking, dryers humming.

Adam, Ramone, and Samuel were carving their paths. Jodie moved between homes, her laughter threading both spaces.

Then I met Rick—at thirty-nine, through mutual friends, at an Irish pub in Chantilly, Virginia.

His charm drowned what my body knew. From the start, something felt off—forced laughter, restless eyes that never settled.

The pub reeked of cigarette smoke. A waitress passed, glasses clinking on her tray.

"Last call on wings!" she shouted over the noise.

Two men argued over a pool shot in the corner.

"That was clean," one said.

"Clean? You nearly took my hand off."

Someone at the bar called out for another round.

"I've got you—hold your horses," the bartender yelled back.

Old beer and fried grease filled the air. Chairs scraped.

Rick fit into that chaos too easily—loud drinking, his laugh cracking through the room, demanding attention. Others mistook it for charm.

A warning settled in me.

A few weeks later, Rick called.

His voice was smooth, confident—almost too practiced.

"I got your number from your friends," he said.

"Oh." I paused. "They didn't mention that."

"Well," he chuckled, "I figured I'd take my shot. Dinner?"

Against my better judgment, I agreed.

After dinner, he was too drunk to drive. The sour smell of beer clung to him, his words sliding around each other.

"You can take the couch for tonight," I told him.

At the time, I was balancing everything—running my salon from home, driving a school bus, raising kids, stitching our life together with whatever strength I had left.

The next morning, I asked him to lock up before I left for my bus shift.

When I returned, he was there—sprawled on my couch, television blaring, shoes kicked off.

"Why are you still here?" I asked.

He didn't look up.

"Hanging out."

"I asked you to leave."

That morning was the first trespass.

Before I understood what was happening, he was staying more nights than he wasn't.

A toothbrush appeared in my bathroom.

Then shoes by the door. A jacket over the back of my favorite chair—

each item arriving quietly, as though it belonged.

One morning, I said,

"Do you need to grab your things before work?"

He shrugged.

"I'm here."

Just like that, he moved in—not with a conversation, but with a shrug. Rick's attention turned suffocating—constant calls, constant watching.

I began doubting instincts I once trusted.

His moods shifted with each drink—calm and soft-spoken, then jagged and unpredictable.

His charm could mask it—for a moment.

It showed up when he brushed off my needs, crossed boundaries, and ignored my children.

The drinking grew heavier. His disregard for everything I valued sharpened.

Then came the letter.

A plain envelope sat on the kitchen counter, addressed to him. I opened it without thinking.

He was married.

When he walked in, I held the paper out, my hand

trembling.

"You lied to me," I whispered.

"You lied right to my face."

He didn't even glance at it.

"It's nothing," he said, brushing past me.

"You're married."

My voice barely rose above breath.

He smirked, as if the truth were temporary.

His uninvited presence invaded my work and my children.

The boundaries I once held collapsed. My children felt it first.

When Rick met my children—Adam, Samuel, and Ramone—something in them went still.

Adam's politeness tightened. Ramone watched him too closely. Samuel stopped joking.

Jodie—twelve—quieted, as if she'd heard something the rest of us missed.

"Mom, he's using you," they said.

"We're not trying to fight you," Adam added quietly.

"We're trying to protect you."

I shook my head.

"You're wrong," I said.

"You're misjudging him."

I didn't want them to see it in me.

The tension pressed in.

One night, after Jodie came home from her dad's, she tried to tell me about her day. She barely got a sentence out before Rick cut across her voice.

"Stop with the drama," he snapped.

"If I want drama, I'll watch Lifetime."

"I... I was telling Mom about my day," Jodie whispered.

She didn't argue after that.

Rick brought his sixteen-year-old son, Lyle, into my home, and the fragile balance snapped.

There was something in him that echoed his father—quiet, watchful, harder to read than it should have been.

While I was working with a client in the salon, Lyle came storming down the stairs, frustration spilling ahead of him.

"I can't take him anymore," he muttered, pacing.

"He drinks, he yells, and somehow it's always my fault."

He had no idea Rick was home—standing out of sight, listening.

"What did you say?" Rick's voice boomed from the doorway.

His son froze, the color draining from his face.

"It's the truth," Lyle said quietly.

Rick lunged. Yelling erupted through the salon, his rage shattering everything.

He grabbed Lyle by the shirt and shoved him out the door so hard the slam rattled the mirrors.

My clients gasped, hands flying to their mouths. One of them stepped forward.

"Please—stop," she said softly.

Rick whirled on her.

"Get out," he barked, rage still pulsing.

"All of you—out!"

They scrambled toward the exit. The familiar scents—shampoo, hairspray, coffee forgotten on the counter—rose around me. None of it settled my spirit. A month later, shaken from the chaos in my salon, Rick took me to Signal Hill Park.

The trails were quiet, the trees bare, the air suspended.

He stopped under a skeletal tree and pulled out a ring.

"Say yes," he murmured.

It wasn't a question.

The ring gleamed cold in his hand.

I was too tired to fight.

I nodded.

A few weeks later, I met his father, Larry Sr. He greeted me with a polite smile and a warm handshake. His kindness was steady—so unlike Rick's volatile charm. We talked easily, though his eyes stayed guarded, as if choosing each word with care.

Rick shot him a look sharp enough to slice the air.

I didn't understand then the tension between them—old, buried under years they never spoke of. Weeks later, I learned Rick had threatened his father to keep quiet about his past. The bitterness between them wasn't a crack; it was a canyon.

I saw it. I didn't act.

New Jersey was safe, familiar, and close to my family.

Having them there mattered.

The image of a beautiful wedding meant more than the truth before me.

On the wedding day, excitement never came—only obligation, heavy as the dress on my shoulders.

Afterward, instead of a honeymoon, I lay next to a man who was a stranger.

That night, tears slipped silently down my cheeks, soaking the pillow.

I should have walked away.

The truth hit me like a fist: I had made my bed. Now I would have to lie in it.

A few days after the wedding, my son Samuel came to do his laundry. He didn't have a washer or dryer.

Rick snapped at him, said he couldn't come into my home freely.

Samuel spat in his face and left.

A month after the ceremony, Rick's father called.

His voice trembled.

"You're Rick's fifth wife," he said softly.

"He's done this before—marrying women with money, draining them dry, then moving on."

"You're next."

A cold weight settled.

When I confronted Rick later, my voice shook with fury.

"Your father told me everything. Am I another name on the list of women you've hurt?"

He didn't flinch.

"He's trying to cause trouble," Rick snapped.

The coldness in his eyes told me more truth.

A year later, he floated the idea of moving to South Carolina—a fresh start: sunlight, ocean air, a new beginning to wash everything clean.

He was careful with his tone, smoothing it the way he did when he wanted leverage.

"You've always loved Myrtle Beach," he said.

"It'll fix everything. You'll see."

He knew Myrtle Beach held pieces of my heart.

To seal the move, he promised to stay behind in Virginia—to manage my home, maintain the two rental properties, and visit every two weeks so I could focus on building my salon. His voice warmed with practiced reassurance, and I wanted to believe him.

"Please, Mom, don't do this," my children begged.

"He wants to take you away from us."

Their fear sat between us.

I brushed it aside once again, choosing hope over what my body already knew.

I found a real estate agent online. Rick and I drove to South Carolina to meet her. We toured property after property—the kind that looked fine on paper but felt hollow the moment we stepped in.

Then we discovered Market Common in Myrtle Beach—a bright, walkable community with the perfect work/live setup.

Home above. Salon and retail below. The place felt carved out for me.

"This could be it," the agent said, gesturing toward

the windows.

I stepped into the picture—clients settling into my chair, the low hum of conversation drifting through the room.

I let myself believe again.

The agent handled everything—finding a lender, securing a law firm, smoothing the path until all I had to do was show up. I poured my savings into the property, choosing faith over fear.

When it came time to sign the papers, Mike, the loan officer, explained the catch.

"We'll need Rick's name on the mortgage," he said. "Yours will go on the deed."

I didn't have a full-time job; I had my salon and school bus shifts. When he slid the papers toward me, the pen weighed.

"Sign here," Mike said, tapping the page.

I signed.

Only later would I understand what that signature cost me.

After closing, I flew to California to collaborate with a company specializing in custom designs and furniture.

I wanted a salon that breathed—soft lighting, warm woods, touches of luxury that whispered welcome.

I hired Bill, a local contractor with experienced hands and a kind voice. Together, we shaped the upstairs and the salon into a place that worked.

When the last coat of paint dried, I packed my life into boxes and moved south, ready to start fresh.

Settling into Myrtle Beach felt like stepping into sunlight after years of gray. Salt air filled my lungs.

My salon thrived from the moment it opened—scissors clicking, dryers humming, the register chiming a steady reassurance that I had made the right choice.

I auditioned as a temporary volunteer co-anchor on Carolina and Company Live with Cecil Chandler. The studio lights carried their own charge, a sharp contrast to the ocean breeze outside.

At the same time, I was filming Hyundai commercials, my face flashing across the screen.

I had earned it.

WMBF News began featuring my salon every Wednesday, spotlighting my work to the community.

Every door opened—until it didn't.

I had six clients from Virginia who made a special trip on a Sunday just for me.

The salon was empty—a day just for them.

Then the door slammed open.

Rick stormed in, already yelling—his voice cutting through the room. My clients froze, hands mid-air.

"Everyone out," he barked, pointing toward the door.

No one moved at first. Then he stepped forward, rage spilling over.

"All of you out!"

Chairs scraped. Capes dropped. My clients gathered their things, shaken, confused—pushed out of a place they had come so far to be.

I stood there as he drove them out of my salon. I had seen this before.

I called the police. That's when Rick began to

unravel. The attention lit something volatile in him.

His jealousy smoldered, then flared.

One evening, during one of his weekend visits, after a long day at the salon, exhaustion pulling at every muscle, I climbed the stairs expecting nothing more than sleep.

Instead, I found Rick sitting on the edge of the bed, his face buried in his hands. The room pressed in.

He looked up, eyes glassy.

"I lost my job," he said.

"I need you. I can't stay up there alone."

His tone was too rehearsed. My stomach tightened as I stepped out of the room and called his boss, the click of the receiver echoing in the quiet.

"Rick left," his boss said flatly.

"Walked out. Didn't say a word."

Each sentence landed.

I overlooked Rick's neglect of my Virginia properties. He never collected rent or paid the mortgages, letting them slide into foreclosure.

When the notices arrived, they landed hard.

The envelopes proved it.

The idea for Crepe Creations Café began in my Virginia home, but it came alive on a trip to Paris, where I was captivated by the charm of crepes—simple, elegant, joyful. I began to imagine a café of my own.

On the drive to Myrtle Beach, Adam and I turned the idea over, testing names out loud until one fit.

By the time we crossed the state line, we had it—Crepe Creations Café.

That dream didn't sit idle.

I traveled to different states studying crepe cafés—

their menus, pricing, traffic flow, and margins. I took notes. Asked questions. Watched what sold and what didn't.

Every detail went onto paper.

I opened Crepe Creations three doors down from my salon in Market Common.

I invested my savings and salon profits into a retail space a few doors down.

I designed the logo, crafted the menu, and perfected each crepe until it felt right.

My salon clients became taste testers.

I promoted the café on radio and TV until the doors opened and customers came through.

Watching Crepe Creations thrive filled me with pride.

It wasn't just a café.

It was something I was building for my boys—something that could one day be theirs.

When Rick told me he had lost his job, I let him step in to run it.

He hadn't built it.

He hadn't funded it.

He hadn't even liked crepes.

I showed him how to spread the batter thin without tearing it.

How to turn them.

How to smile at customers about flavors he never ordered himself.

The café opened strong—morning rushes, afternoon regulars. It was my money, my vision, my work.

For a while, it held.

But outside those walls, he told a different story.

"She wanted a convertible, so I bought her a convertible," "She wanted to move, so we moved."

Laughter. Nods. Someone clapped him on the back.

I stood there, listening as my history was reassigned.

Later, walking past the lit storefronts, I stopped.

"Stop lying to people," I said.

"Especially in front of me."

He shrugged.

"I'm just talking."

"No," I said.

"You're not talking. You're lying."

He smiled—thin and dismissive.

As my success grew, so did Rick's resentment.

Six months after the café opened, clients began pulling me aside, voices low, telling me they'd seen him—once, then again—kissing another woman.

I said little, filed it away, waiting for proof I didn't want. It didn't take long.

One morning, after he hadn't come home the night before, I walked into the café expecting to find him working.

Instead, I stepped into ankle-deep water.

Chairs floated. Cords soaked. The air smelled damp, sour—ruined. The water had taken the floor.

"This wasn't an accident," I whispered.

Rick had been gone for an entire week—not working, not helping—living with his mistress, "Emma."

The flooding and his disappearance aligned too

cleanly.

Emma—owner of a school of healthy living.

Rick—an alcoholic, a chain smoker.

One morning, a client pulled me aside, her eyes wide—no longer warning me, only confirming what I already knew.

"Halaina... I saw him," she whispered.

"He was kissing her. I'm so sorry."

Her voice trembled—and that tenderness cut deeper than the betrayal itself.

By then, everything was already breaking.

Jodie—craving solid ground beneath her feet—decided to move in with me in Myrtle Beach.

She wanted stability. A fresh start. A chance for us to finally be mother and daughter without interference.

Rick had already left his mark.

What he called love was a slow drip—

a comment, a look, then a correction that wasn't one.

Each one small. Deliberate.

Jodie grew quieter around him.

He'd been fracturing us from the beginning—pulling me away until distance did the rest.

When she chose me, I should have protected that.

Instead, I kept trying to manage him.

He sent me texts about my own daughter—sexual, slanderous, meant to humiliate.

A grown man reducing a teenage girl to something obscene.

The cost wasn't financial. It was my daughter.

One night, I finally stood up to him.

It started with Jodie. The tension had been

building—the way he chipped at her until the house felt tight.

He told her she needed to leave.

Something in me shifted.

"No," I said.

That's when he moved.

He walked out onto the balcony without a word.

I followed.

He had gathered our wedding photos—every one of them—and started lighting them on fire.

The flames caught quickly, curling the edges, faces disappearing in the heat.

He stood there, burning them one by one, watching.

I didn't try to stop him.

I just watched.

Not because I cared about the pictures.

The final humiliation came during a trip to Cancun with Jodie and my salon manager.

The turquoise water sparkled—calm, clear, untouched.

For a moment, it seemed to offer peace.

My body didn't believe it.

Before we left, I changed the locks on the salon. My briefcase held everything—business records, personal documents, the backbone of my new beginning.

Turning that key reclaimed one small piece of my life.

On the flight to Cancun, sunlight warmed my face. Unease settled in me.

Below, the water opened in bands of color—pale

green at the shore, deepening into blue so clear it looked lit from within. White sand traced the edge like a line drawn by hand.

The beauty stretched wide and endless, untouched by anything waiting for me on the ground.

"Mom, relax," Jodie whispered, resting her head against the window.

"I'm trying," I murmured, though every nerve stayed braced.

Even thousands of miles away, he stayed inside me.

I carried him like thorns under my skin.

It was time to stop fixing him.

It was time to free myself.

On the second day of our trip, the hotel room was quiet—the kind that lets your guard drop for half a breath.

Then the phone rang.

"Halaina, are you okay?" a client asked.

"I saw your Facebook post. What's going on?"

My stomach dropped.

"What post?"

The silence on the other end told me everything before she spoke.

Rick—reckless, calculating—hacked my Facebook account.

He posted it in my name.

Attacking me, my business, my reputation.

Each post was personal. Deliberate. Aimed to wound where I was raw.

We caught the first flight home.

When I opened the door, the smell hit me first—stale alcohol, sweat, something sharp and broken in the air.

The living room looked as though violence had passed through. Furniture overturned. Glass scattered. Drawers gutted.

Then the salon.

The lock hung splintered—broken open. My briefcase was gone.

My salon manager had arrived earlier. She left her luggage at the door and came to pick us up from the airport.

The house reeked of alcohol. Drawers yawning open. Furniture shoved crooked out of place.

Rick's betrayal flooded my mind. Nicholas's betrayal followed close behind.

Another man who promised loyalty and delivered destruction—another storm I had let into my home.

My body recognized the pattern before my mind could argue it.

I called the police, again.

Their radios crackled as they moved through the house.

They checked every room. Every corner.

Time stretched, heavy and unreal.

Later, one of the officers spotted him near the dumpsters behind the building.

They went digging through the trash.

They found my briefcase.

They found my manager's luggage.

And they found Rick.

He was stumbling drunk, eyes glassy, anger leaking

out of him.

"You can't stop me," he slurred as they pulled him away.

"None of you can."

His words hung in the air long after the patrol car disappeared.

Relief settled over me—thin and incomplete.

With Rick in jail, I changed the locks.

The click of the new deadbolt marked the first clean boundary I had set in years.

The illusion didn't last.

He returned to the café without warning, his presence alone reopening every wound he'd carved. And when he wasn't there, his messages were—the texts came one after another, sharp and venomous, not meant to argue but to erode. Then came the final blow.

Outside my front door were the antique dolls I'd bought long before Rick.

I had placed them there as a welcome because they resembled my parents.

He had destroyed them.

Porcelain limbs hacked off. Tiny rocking chairs splintered.

I couldn't breathe.

Those dolls had survived every move, every hardship, every chapter of my life.

Now they lay scattered at my feet.

I called the police once more.

"The security cameras should help deter future

damage," they said.

Deter. The word landed uselessly.

The cameras recorded the aftermath.

They couldn't undo the ache beneath my ribs or the silence that settled into Jodie.

Anger rose.

I wanted to make Rick and Emma pay.

I wanted the weight of everything they'd done to crush them the way it had crushed me.

Instead, he came to me calmly, as if this were reasonable.

"If you sign the café over to me," he said,

"I'll sign the mortgage over to you."

I believed him.

Everything tied to that house fell on me—just as it always had.

I signed the café over and kept paying the mortgage.

He never signed it back.

By the time I understood what he had done, the loss was already sealed.

The house was gone. My salon followed. The café was the last thing standing—and he stripped that too.

He and Emma presented it as their creation.

One morning, my phone lit up.

I opened Facebook.

There it was.

A post announcing that he and Emma had "created" Crepe Creations Café.

Their dream. Their vision.

Photos of the space I had paid for. The counters I had chosen. The menu I had built.

My work—reframed as theirs.

I stared at the screen, heat rushing to my face.

Losing the café had already taken the ground from under me.

This took my voice with it.

I responded once. Calm. Factual. Brief.

He deleted it within minutes.

Just like that, the lie stood—polished, public, intact—while I watched my life rewritten.

Erasure.

Years later, another client called.

"Halaina... Emma... Rick's wife passed away."

The words hung in the air—final and cold.

I felt no relief, no joy—only stillness.

The kind that comes when God closes a chapter no human hands could.

Revenge wasn't mine to carry.

He took Crepe Creations, piece by piece.

I stopped going to Market Common.

I couldn't walk past those windows and watch my life behind the glass.

The café ended for me the day he turned it into leverage.

Time moved forward without me. I built a new life around it—until one day, a client came in for her appointment.

"I drove by Crepe Creations."

She paused.
"It's closed."
His wife died.
The café went under.
I never got back what was taken.
I got back myself.
And I'm still here.

Chapter 20

MOTHER ROOT

"She is clothed with strength and dignity;
she can laugh at the days to come."
(Proverbs 31:25, NIV)

Before the next chapter, I stood still long enough to look back.

Motherhood did not begin with readiness. It began in a damp basement that smelled of mildew, light thin and yellow against concrete walls. That was where it found me—below ground, air heavy and still.

I used to press my back against those walls when the weight of it got too heavy. The concrete was always cold. It never warmed to me. Neither did the fear.

I was barely more than a girl, learning in the same breath how to give birth and how to survive. My hands were young. My voice shook. I held babies before I understood how to hold my own fear.

There were nights I lay on my back, staring at the ceiling, listening for three rhythms of breathing from three rooms. I counted them. One. Two. Three. If they were breathing, I could rest.

I did not grow up wrapped in tenderness. Love was not

handed to me gently.

I learned it by doing—packing lunches before sunrise, scrubbing stains from school shirts, stretching grocery money across weeks that felt too long. It lived in apologies whispered through closed doors. In the quiet after they slept. Lying awake, wondering if I had already made mistakes I couldn't undo.

Fear pressed behind my ribs—failing them, becoming what had wounded me, the world reaching them before I could stand in front of it.

Raising three boys alone meant hearing how loud the world could be. I saw how quickly it tried to harden them. Shoulders squared too early. Fists clenched when words would have served better.

Raising a girl meant something else. It meant feeling her eyes on me when I thought she wasn't looking. Knowing she would learn what love looked like by watching what I accepted—or refused.

There were moments I failed—my voice was sharp, patience thin, doors closing harder than they should have. I stayed in places that dimmed us. I left before I understood the cost.

Still, every morning, I rose. Coffee poured into chipped mugs, backpacks zipped, shoes by the door, hair braided, hands held in parking lots.

I prayed more than I slept. I bargained with God in kitchens lit by stove light—asking for protection, for wisdom, for one more day.

He always gave it to me. Morning always came. I learned to treat that as an answer.

I did not want anything extraordinary for my kids.

I wanted ordinary without fear. Doors that opened without bracing. Laughter that didn't stop when footsteps entered the room.

When I look at my children—grown, carrying lives of their own—I do not see perfection. I see resilience shaped in small, stubborn moments.

They were not raised by a flawless mother. They were raised by a woman who fought.

We were not polished—only present, roots pressed into whatever ground we were given.

Through noise and leaving and rebuilding, through nights that felt endless and mornings that came too fast, we held.

I stayed.

And they rose.

Chapter 21

RECLAIMED SOIL

"By their fruit you will recognize them."
(Matthew 7:16, NIV)

I stayed. Long enough to notice what remained.

I wasn't bracing or running. My days were full, my evenings my own. I wasn't looking for anyone.

A friend suggested online dating, and I resisted at first.

One night, curled on the couch with the television murmuring in the background, I created a profile and set the phone beside me.

Minutes later, it began chiming. Again. And again. I stared at the screen, startled by the attention, unsure what to do with it.

I scrolled through message after message—some sincere, others careless, ignoring what I had made clear.

I almost closed the app. Turned off the lamp. Let the night go quiet again.

Andy entered my life without force.

No urgency. No heat. I was living in a townhome at

the time. The day we met, I had spent the afternoon at the beach, still in my swimsuit beneath a loose dress, sand clinging to my feet. I remember thinking, if someone couldn't meet me like this, they didn't belong in my life.

We met at LongHorn Steakhouse, and hours passed without notice. Chairs were stacked. Staff swept around us. We didn't move.

He made me laugh in a way that surprised me—the kind that comes from the belly, not the nerves.

"I can't believe it's this late," I said.

"I don't want to leave yet," he answered.

Neither did I.

We fell into a rhythm—movies on the couch, weekends outdoors, quiet drives where nothing needed explaining. We never fought—not once. Not over small things. Not over anything. Andy was the first person I truly loved. Being with him felt easy in a way I hadn't known before.

His family welcomed me easily. Plates were pressed into my hands. Seats were pulled out without asking. Laughter bounced off their walls, the clatter of forks filling the room. I sat among them at ease.

Not long after, he invited me to a campground where his parents were camping. Motorhomes formed a loose circle beneath tall pines. Folding chairs gathered around the fire. Smoke lifted into the dark, carrying the scent of burning wood. His mother handed me a plate before I could refuse. His father nodded once, like that was enough. No one asked anything. They just made room at the table.

Because I loved that feeling, I traded my Nissan Murano for a motorhome and never looked back. Camping stopped being something I visited. It became mine.

He came with me when he could—weekends in South Carolina campgrounds, his camera always in his hands.

He took pictures of everything—the trees, the light, me when I wasn't looking.

We walked the campground at dusk, passing other sites and exchanging quiet hellos that sometimes turned into stories.

Two years later, because I loved cooking for us under the stars, I traded for a newer, larger motorhome with an outdoor kitchen and a small television mounted outside next to it.

Nights gathered around us—the soft crackle of a nearby fire, the low murmur of other campers, the scent of food rising into the open air. I cooked while he lingered close, camera never far from his hands. We ate outside, plates warm in our laps, the sky stretched wide above us—the kind of peace you don't question.

Belonging didn't ache here. It existed. Camping became our refuge. Smoke curled from the fire pit, clinging to our clothes long after the flames died down. Mornings smelled of strong-brewed coffee and sizzling bacon on the outdoor grills.

He introduced me to kayaking, something I would never have tried on my own. I feared the water; beside him, I learned to trust my balance. We paddled through narrow inlets, saying little, the water carrying us forward.

Once, on Edisto Beach—Shell Island, where the

shoreline was scattered with shells—I knelt in the sand and uncovered a perfect sand dollar, cool and fragile against my palm, grains slipping through my fingers. Gulls drifted overhead, their calls carried on the wind as the tide moved in and out beside me.

We spent hours hunting for shark teeth, sitting beneath the golden sun, sifting through the sand like it might give something back. It felt like treasure hunting. We were never bored.

"Look at this," I said, brushing it clean.

Andy smiled.

"You always find the good stuff."

I kept it.

At home, the days slowed. The garage filled with sawdust and varnish, the whine of tools echoing against concrete. Wood shavings dusted the floor as we worked side by side. Evenings ended with movies and quiet closeness, the TV's low glow flickering across the walls.

Andy was a graphic designer—something we shared. He designed ads for our T-shirts and websites, and we worked well together. He even helped me with my salon ads. He had a creative eye.

Ease didn't announce its exit.

It shifted slowly.

I handled the meals, the house, the plans, and the bills. Andy settled into what I carried. I noticed it first in small things—unfinished meals, tasks assumed rather than shared. I washed the dishes again. I fixed the leaky faucet myself. I filled the gaps without a word.

One night, exhausted, I left the dishes in the sink—plates from the meal I had cooked for him still stacked by the stove.

I went to work the next morning. When I came home that evening, the dirty dishes were still there.

I stood in the doorway looking at them. Then at him. The room held everything we hadn't said.

So was Andy.

"Did you get any breaks today?" I asked.

"Yes. A few," he said.

I was furious.

"I can't keep doing everything," I said softly.

His answer was simple.

"I'll spend the night and leave in the morning."

It shocked me.

I had left before—more than once—and gone back. What followed wasn't a fight. It was a pause—heavy, unmoving, louder than words.

Before we ended it, he made a video of the house to help it sell. I was grateful for that. My townhome sold within two weeks, and I bought a house with a wide driveway for my motorhome. The keys were cool and heavy in my hand the day I closed.

I left without anger, without drama. Loving him showed me what it looked like when things worked—and what it costs when it isn't shared.

Later, I learned he had been unfaithful.

He had always insisted he wasn't that kind of man.

Relief walked out with me.

When Andy married two years later, I wished him well and meant it.

During COVID, when campgrounds closed and the world shut down, I sold the motorhome. When my life opened again, I bought another.

The road had never belonged to him. It belonged to me.

I still travel alone now. I camp in silence, cook beneath open sky, and wake without answering to anyone. What began beside him, I carried forward on my own.

I gave myself time. Not enough, maybe. But I tried.

Kurt came later—wrapped in stories polished by loss.

I met him through social media just before Christmas of 2022. We agreed to meet at Outback Steakhouse. Over dinner, he spoke easily about loss, survival, and the life he had endured.

When I stepped inside his home, the air was stale—dishes stacked in the sink. Dust stuck in the corners. The life he described and the life he lived did not match. Something in me pulled back.

"God kept me alive for a reason," he said.

"Take me home," I said quietly.

The next day, I told him I couldn't continue. Our lives did not align. He did not let go easily.

I should have stopped there. Instead, compassion took hold. He said his son needed me—that the boy asked for me by name.

I told myself I could make a difference.

Eight months into the relationship, his landlord told him to leave. Instead of finding somewhere else to go, he stayed. I let him and Zabe move in with me.

My clean rooms changed. The air grew stale. Clutter crept into corners.

He called me Yamma—his word for mom. He introduced me that way to everyone. I taught him how to cook—eggs, grilled cheese—small things that mattered to him.

Kurt helped around the house. It didn't change the feeling I had. The drinking worsened. Beer cans rattled in the garage late into the night. I kept trying to fix what was never mine to fix.

I had bought the boat believing it would give us something to share.

One night on the water, after he had been drinking, the boat cut too close to the trees, branches tearing at my arms.

"This isn't funny," I snapped.

"We're fine," he slurred.

Another time, he drove with an open beer in his hand—with Zabe in the car.

One morning, I woke to the sound of liquid hitting plastic. At first, I thought it was raining. When I opened my eyes, Kurt was standing in the room, drunk, urinating on the floor.

Then came the saddest day of my life—the day I lost Chico.

"Where's Chico?"

"He's outside," Zabe said.

I already knew.

It had been a brutally hot day.

I drove as fast as I could, one hand on the wheel,

talking to him the way you talk to someone you're not sure can still hear you.

By the time we arrived, it was already over.

I held his collar afterward. The leather was warm from my hand.

That was all I had left.

"I'm sorry, Yamma," he said, his voice breaking. "I didn't mean to hurt Chico."

I pulled him into me, his body shaking against mine.

Kurt's stories surfaced quickly. They fractured—then collapsed. After his brother and sister-in-law visited, I called her. She told me the truth. He had never served overseas. Never had leukemia. When I confronted him, he denied it. A week later, he confessed.

By then, my life had shrunk to the walls of my bedroom. I stayed there most days, trying to get through it.

He said he deserved part of the boat. I gave him $3,000 to help him move on—to make it easier for him to leave.

Zabe collapsed into me, crying so hard he could barely speak.

"I don't want to go," he said. "I want to stay with you."

"I love you, Yamma."

I held him, arms wrapped tight, and said nothing.

I could not save him without losing myself.

I didn't need a project. I needed a partner.

I saw it clearly then—what someone does will always

reveal who they are. I would never confuse the two again. The house felt lighter after they left.

For weeks, the rooms echoed with absence. I missed the footsteps, the soft laughter that had followed me from room to room.

Standing alone in my kitchen one evening, the sink finally empty, the counters bare, I understood how long I had mistaken effort for love.

For the first time in years, the house was quiet—and I was not afraid of it.

I had already crossed an ocean to meet it.

Chapter 22

My Roots, My Garden

"He restores my soul."
(Psalm 23:3, NIV)

A quiet settled into the house long before I was ready for it. Not grief. Not vigilance. Something steadier.

Afternoon light crossed the floor. The air no longer braced.

For most of my life, I mistook motion for survival.

When the movement stopped, I didn't know who I was without it.

The light shifted. I didn't follow.

Time passed. For once, I stayed.

I found a place where the doors didn't slam and the walls didn't echo.

Silver Creek gave me room to breathe.

Jodie claimed the larger bedroom without hesitation. The certainty was already in her voice. She walked to school while I drove to the salon in the mornings, the air warm, the days ordinary in the best way.

I unlocked the door, swept the floor, and brewed the coffee. Brushes lined up where I left them. Clients returned. Laughter came back in small waves.

The business grew. So did the space in me.

The church became a place where I could sit without having to perform strength.

Counseling gave me language I had never learned—boundaries, patterns, permission to rest. I wasn't becoming someone new. I was shedding what no longer belonged.

I went to Ramallah.

The flight was long. The city felt ancient beneath my feet—stone and dust and something older than any name I had for it. I hadn't known how much the distance had been costing me until I closed it.

I stood at Baba's grave and said what had waited too long to be said.

The wind moved through the trees. No one hurried me. Some things don't need witnesses to be finished.

I left in peace.

I thought I had finished saying goodbye.

Yamma's absence lingered. She died while I was unraveling with Rick—moving between chaos and obligation, flying back and forth to New Jersey just to be with her. Every trip took its toll; I never questioned it. Being with her mattered more than anything I was leaving behind.

When she died, it broke something open in me. I sobbed for months—deep, uncontrollable grief that didn't move on a schedule. It still comes. It still catches me without warning.

Time moved forward, even when I hadn't.

After I bought my home in Carolina Lakes, my brother Ibrahim came to stay for a few days.

It was the Fourth of July. I took him to Broadway at the Beach, and he was so happy.

Fireworks cracked overhead, loud and sudden, echoing across the water. The bursts came one after another, lighting the sky. The air smelled of smoke and sweetness.

Then he was gone.

I kept thinking about the light on his face that night. How happy he had been. How I hadn't known to hold it longer.

The timing felt cruel. I had just begun to feel stable. Grief came all at once, layered and relentless, and I didn't know how to hold it.

Ibrahim had seen every version of me—the excesses, the failures, the seasons where I barely held myself together. And in the end, he saw me rise.

I didn't know our last goodbye would be the last.

His death didn't shatter me. It hollowed me, leaving a quiet space where grief and love lived side by side. Survival had carried me this far—but peace?

It remained out of reach.

On top of everything else, Adam's silence stretched longer than I knew how to bear.

Grandchildren grew through photographs instead of touch.

Some nights I prayed. Some nights I just breathed. Both counted.

My motorhome wasn't an escape. It was proof that movement was finally my choice. I could go when I wanted, stop when I needed, sleep beneath an open sky without running.

The house gave me roots. The road reminded me I still had wings.

In July, my phone rang.

"Hi, Teta."

The call dropped before I could speak.

It rang again.

"Teta, it's Noah. I'm at your front door."

I pulled up the camera, heart hammering, afraid to trust my own eyes. There he stood—taller than memory, broader through the shoulders, unmistakably mine.

I left the beach without thinking, sand clinging to my feet, salt drying against my skin. I drove home through tears I didn't bother wiping away. When I pulled into the driveway, he was waiting.

"Teta," he said again.

I reached him before he finished. His arms were solid. Honest. Warm. My cheek pressed against his shoulder. He smelled like sun and laundry and something newly his.

The years collapsed without explanation.

We sat with sunlight spilling across the floor, plates of food forgotten as we talked—not about what was lost, about whom he was becoming.

A week later, Bria arrived.

She ran into my arms as if nothing had ever broken. Backpacks returned to the hallway. Laughter filled the rooms. The quiet didn't disappear—it softened, made room.

Adam followed. We spoke without circling the past, without pretending it hadn't hurt—just staying long enough to hear each other through. No rehearsed apologies. Just presence.

We drove to Charleston and sat by the water with salt in the air and sunlight trembling across the surface. Boats drifted. Children laughed. Nothing needed fixing.

Months later, I traveled to Maryland to visit Adam.

Before I left, I went to see Lina.

We sat together and spoke about old times—about the life that had carried us in different ways.

I made things right between us. Not out of obligation—but because it was time.

We didn't linger in the past. We honored it, and let it rest.

And in that letting go, something quiet followed.

It did not come with thunder. Not with spectacle. It came like this.

That night, the sink was empty.

The counters were clear.

The house rested—the way I had learned to rest—without vigilance, without fear.

I had crossed oceans. I had buried the dead. I had survived the breaking.

I built a life. I found moments of peace.
And still—some nights, the past comes for me.
I have nightmares.
About Nicholas.
About my ex-husbands.
About my sister.
About my mother and father.
They come without asking. Without warning.
They remind me of everything I have lived through.
But morning still comes.
And when it does, I am still here.
Still rooted.
Still choosing peace—again, and again, and again.
My soil is reclaimed.
My garden is still growing—even in the dark.

AFTERWARD

If you are reading this, something in this story found you.

Maybe you recognized a room you once lived in. A voice that sounded familiar. A version of yourself you've been trying to outrun or understand or forgive.

I wrote this book because I needed to say what happened. Not to assign blame. Not to perform survival. But because the truth of a life deserves to be spoken out loud — and because silence, I learned, is its own kind of loss.

If you have ever felt stuck, I want you to know something: stuck is not the same as finished. I stayed in places that cost me years. I gave chances that were never earned. I carried weight that was never mine to carry. And still — I am here. Still choosing. Still growing.

The most important thing this life has taught me — the lesson I wish someone had handed me early, wrapped plainly, without apology — is this:

What someone does will always reveal who they are.

Not what they say. Not what they promise in the warmth of a new beginning. Not the story they tell about themselves at dinner, or the version they perform for the people watching.

What they do. Quietly. Consistently. When they think

you're not paying attention.

I spent too many years listening to words instead of watching actions. I confused charm for character. Compassion for wisdom. Effort for love.

I am not ashamed of that. I was learning. We are always learning.

But I want you to learn it sooner than I did.

Trust what you see. Trust the feeling that settles in your body before your mind has found the language for it. Trust the quiet voice that speaks up before you have talked yourself out of listening.

That voice is not fear. It is knowledge. It is every version of yourself that has already lived through something and survived it.

You are allowed to rest. You are allowed to take up space. You are allowed to want a life that feels like yours — not a life built around managing someone else's chaos, or shrinking yourself to make room for someone who was never going to fill the space anyway.

I have been broken open. I have buried people I loved. I have stood in rooms where everything I built had been taken, and I have had to decide, in those rooms, whether I was going to stay on the floor or get up.

I always got up.

Not because I was fearless. Because I was rooted.

My roots held even when I couldn't see them. Even when the ground felt like nothing. Even in the dark.

If you are lost right now — if you are in a season that feels like it has no end — I am not going to tell you it gets easier. I am going to tell you something truer:

You get stronger. And morning keeps coming.

This story is mine. But the survival in it belongs to anyone who has ever had to choose themselves — quietly, without applause, in a room where no one was watching.

That is the bravest thing a person can do.

Thank you for reading. Thank you for trusting me with your time.

I hope something in these pages found the part of you that needed to hear it.

With love and hard-won peace,

Halaina

From Yamma's Kitchen

Bread with Za'atar

Dough flattened by hand, olive oil pressed into the surface, za'atar scattered generously.

The smell filled the house before it ever reached the table.

We tore it while it was still warm.

Yamma said some things should never be eaten alone.

Mujadara

Lentils and rice, but it was never about the lentils.

It was the onions—fried slowly until they darkened, just shy of burning.

Yamma said that's where the flavor lived.

We ate it quietly, the sweetness of onions lingering longer than anything else.

Labneh

Yogurt left to strain overnight, becoming something thicker, quieter.

Spread across bread, olive oil pressed into it, mint still clinging to the edges.

Wrapped and sent with me without a word.

Later, I'd notice the smell still on my fingers.

Something that stayed longer than it should have.

Grape Leaves

Rice, tomatoes, parsley, olive oil.

Rolled tight between her fingers—scoop, fold, tuck.

If they opened in the pot, she said, you rushed them.

Patience held everything together.

Sambousek

Dough rolled thin, circles pressed from its surface.

Meat spiced without measuring—onion, salt, something warm.

Yamma and her sisters sat close, hands moving faster than the stories between them.

Fold, pinch, seal.

If one opened, it meant you rushed it.

They fried in batches, the smell filling the house before the tray was full.

We never ate the first one alone.

Sfiha

Small rounds of dough topped with spiced meat, baked until the edges crisped.

They came out of the oven one after another, never fast enough.

We ate them standing, talking over each other, reaching before they cooled.

No one counted how many.

Kibbeh

Bulgur and meat pressed together, shaped by hand.

Hollowed, filled, sealed.

Each one carried more than its filling—

time, care, and the quiet expectation that nothing should break.

Maklouba

Rice, meat, vegetables layered carefully in a pot—nothing out of place.

Then the turning.

A breath held.

The whole thing flipped at once—

what was hidden revealed, what was beneath brought to the top.

Mansaf

Lamb and rice laid out wide, jameed poured over everything.

Sharp, fermented, unmistakable.

It wasn't adjusted. It wasn't softened.

It was meant to be exactly what it was.

We stood close, eating from the same place.

No one asked for more. You took what was in front of you.

It tasted older than the room we were in.

Knafeh

Shredded dough, cheese hidden underneath, syrup poured while it's still hot.

It arrived golden, cut into squares that never stayed whole for long.

We burned our fingers reaching for it too soon.

Sweetness like that didn't wait.

Maamoul

Semolina dough pressed around dates or nuts, shaped in carved wooden molds.

Each one held a pattern—small, careful, deliberate.

They were made for holidays, for visits, for people who came and stayed.

Powdered sugar dusted everything, even the spaces between us.

Qatayif

Sundays smelled like qatayif.

Sweet batter, soft and round, left open on one side.

Filled while still warm, folded closed, browned just enough.

The scent moved through the hallway before anyone called us.

We always came anyway.

Some things didn't need to be announced.

Arabic Coffee

Water, coffee, cardamom.

Bitter and sharp, poured into small cups that never filled all the way.

It wasn't meant to satisfy thirst.

It was meant to be shared, slowly, between words.

Glossary

Family Terms

Baba — father

Yamma — mother

Teta — grandmother

Jiddo — grandfather

Khalti — my aunt (maternal aunt)

Khalati — my aunts (maternal aunts)

Amo — uncle (paternal uncle)

Ikhwani — my brothers

Um — mother of; a respectful honorific used before a child's name (e.g., Um Ibrahim — Mother of Ibrahim)

Place & Community

Hara — neighborhood

Harat al-Nasarah — the Christian Quarter

El-Manara — central square in Ramallah

Religious & Spiritual Phrases

Allah — God

Allahu akbar — God is greatest

Inshallah — God willing

Subhan Allah — glory be to God

Ya Allah — oh God

Allah yaster — may God protect us

Allah maakon — God be with you

Allah ybarek fik — God bless you

Adhan — call to prayer

EVERYDAY EXPRESSIONS

Sabah el-khair — good morning

Sabah el-noor — morning light — the response to good morning

Ahlan wa sahlan — welcome

Aywa — yes

Yalla — let's go

Taali — come here

Hona — here

Kefik — how are you

Huwa — he; it is him

TERMS OF ENDEARMENT

Habibi — my love (masculine)

Habibti — my love (feminine)

Ya ibni — my son

Ya qalbi — my heart

Ya rohi — my soul

Ya zaman — oh, what times — an expression of longing

Khatibti — my fiancée

PHRASES

Ana asfa — I'm sorry

Ma kunt aqsid — I didn't mean it

Ishtaqnalak ktir — we missed you so much

Ana kaman ishtaqtillik — I missed you too

Hada ismuki — that's your name

Hadha akhi — this is your brother

Hadi ilik — this is for you

Ursumi eshi jamilan — draw something beautiful

La', mish mumkin — it's not possible

Ya hayawan — you animal — an insult

Ya Um Ibrahim — mother of Ibrahim — honorific title

FOOD & CULTURAL ITEMS

Khubz — bread

Kaak — sesame bread

Kaak hami — hot sesame bread

Za'atar — herb blend of thyme, sesame, and sumac

Labneh — strained yogurt cheese

Hummus — chickpea dip

Baba ghanoush — smoky eggplant dip

Falafel — fried chickpea patties

Mujaddarah — lentils and rice with caramelized onions

Makloubeh — upside-down rice, meat, and vegetable dish

Mansaf — lamb and rice in fermented yogurt sauce

Sfiha — spiced meat flatbread

Sambousek — stuffed fried pastries

Kibbeh — bulgur and meat croquettes

Kanafeh — sweet cheese pastry with syrup

Ma'amoul — stuffed semolina cookies

Qatayif — filled sweet pancakes

Jameed — dried fermented yogurt used in Mansaf

Mazza — small shared dishes served together

Qahwa — Arabic coffee with cardamom

Shay — tea

CULTURAL TERMS

Thob — traditional embroidered dress

Tatreez — Palestinian embroidery

Heta — coin-adorned headpiece

Kanun — coal brazier used for heating

Souk — market

Shisha — hookah

Tabla — hand drum

Dabke — traditional Palestinian group dance

Henna — ceremonial plant dye used for celebrations

Mashlahat — wedding gift bundles of almonds and chocolates

Servees — shared taxi — the main form of public transport in Ramallah

CULTURAL EXPRESSIONS

Zaghareet — celebratory ululation made by women at joyful occasions

Ya — oh; hey — used before a name or term of address

Acknowledgments

This book would not have been possible without the support of my family, friends, clients, and colleagues.

First, my children—you taught me more than I ever expected.

Adam, thank you for your kind heart and enterprising spirit.

Ramone, thank you for your infectious laughter and sarcasm.

Samuel, thank you for your honesty and stubbornness, and for showing me different perspectives, even when we didn't always agree.

Jodie, thank you for your passion and curiosity—your drive to make a difference in the world continues to inspire me.

To my parents and siblings, thank you for shaping who I am.

Baba, your quiet strength was a constant comfort.

Yamma, your resilience—even in the hardest moments—is a lesson I carry every day.

Ibrahim, you were the rock of our family. Your loyalty held us together when everything felt like it was breaking.

Through every trial and triumph, you have been my anchor.

To my clients from Virginia to South Carolina—you became family. Your trust, laughter, and willingness to share your lives with me made this journey possible.

Donna, thank you for believing in me, especially in those early days of building my salon. Your generosity and support carried me forward when I needed it most.

Karen, thank you for planting the seed of this book years ago. Your belief in my story kept me writing, and for that, I am forever grateful.

Finally, to the readers—thank you for being here.
I hope my story encourages you to trust your own strength and embrace whatever path lies ahead.

Reader's Guide

Sit with these questions slowly. Let them meet you where you are—not where you think you should be. There are no right answers here. Only honest ones.

Recognition

Was there a moment in this book where you recognized yourself.

Not a moment you admired from a distance—but one that found you.

What did that recognition feel like.

What did it ask of you.

Silence

Think of something you have carried in silence.

How long have you held it.

How has that silence shaped you—the way you move through rooms, the way you trust, the way you speak or don't.

What might change if you finally gave it a voice.

Origins

Where did you first learn that staying quiet was safer than speaking.

Was it a place, a person, a moment—or something so

woven into your upbringing you couldn't name it.

Halaina carried her silence from Ramallah across an ocean. What have you carried from where you began.

Survival

Describe what survival looked like in the hardest season of your life.

What parts of you did it protect.

What did it cost.

Is there anything survival asked you to give up that you are still grieving.

Loss & Support

Recall a time when everything felt like it was falling apart.

Who stood beside you—and who didn't.

What did you discover about yourself in the absence of the people you expected to stay.

Truth

Has there been a person in your life whose actions told you a truth their words never would.

How long did it take you to trust what you saw over what you were told.

What made the difference.

Resilience

Resilience is often spoken about, but rarely examined.

Where does yours come from.

What has it endured that most people around you don't know about.

Has it ever come at a cost to yourself—and if so, what did that cost look like.

Release

Consider what you have had to release in order to grow.

Not what was taken from you—what you chose to let go.

What are you still holding onto, even now.

What would it feel like to set it down.

Faith & Meaning

In moments of hardship, where—if anywhere—have you found faith or meaning.

Not the kind that comes easily. The kind that costs something to hold onto.

How has your relationship with faith, or the absence of it, shaped the way you move through loss.

Becoming

Your identity is not fixed.

How has adversity reshaped the way you see yourself.

How do you hold space for who you used to be while honoring who you are still becoming.

Is there a version of yourself you have not yet given yourself permission to become.

A Note from Halaina

These questions are not meant to be answered all at once. Some may not be ready for you yet—and that is not a failure. It is information.

Return to the ones that made you pause. Sit longest with the ones that made you uncomfortable. Those are usually the ones with something waiting inside them.

You don't have to have it all figured out to begin. You just have to be willing to be honest—with yourself, and if you're reading this in a group, with each other.

That willingness is where everything starts.

About the Author

Halaina is the author of Resilient Roots, Rooted in Truth, One Land, Two Sides, and Miles From Home. Her work explores family, faith, resilience, belonging, and the stories we inherit.

She grew up in the hills of Ramallah, where life taught her early lessons about endurance, identity, and the quiet strength required to keep moving forward. She carried those lessons across an ocean through motherhood, loss, reinvention, financial hardship, and rebuilding.

What she found on the other side was not a life restored, but something more honest—a life fully her own.

She lives in South Carolina, where she owns a salon, travels alone in a motorhome, and writes the stories she once had no words to tell.

Stay Connected

halaina.com

For new releases, book updates, and contact information

www.ingramcontent.com/pod-product-compliance
Lightning Source LLC
LaVergne TN
LVHW100509110826
845146LV00002B/566

9798994536704